Praise for
Coaching a–z

"We are treated here to a festival of wisdom, insight, and creative practices of dialogue—especially relevant for therapists, counselors, and coaches, but indeed for thriving in all our daily relations. A joy to read."
KENNETH J. GERGEN, PhD, president, Taos Institute; author, *Relational Being: Beyond Self and Community*

"Haesun Moon is an accomplished coach and trainer. Here, she describes the Solution-Focused techniques she uses in conversations with others by sharing personal and professional anecdotes. The result is a forward-looking, competency-based approach to coaching that is persuasive, engaging, and readily understood. Professionals and non-professionals alike will discover much in this book they can usefully carry into their conversations with clients, colleagues, friends, and family."
PETER DE JONG, PhD, MSW, co-author, *Interviewing for Solutions*; professor emeritus, sociology and social work, Calvin University; mental health therapist

T0025736

"Sometimes a book comes along that makes you say, 'WOW, everyone needs this book!' Practical, inspiring, and perspective shifting, *Coaching A–Z: The Extraordinary Use of Ordinary Words* clearly illustrates the power of language and communication to create and to change realities. Grounded in Haesun Moon's meta theory, the Dialogic Orientation Quadrant, the stories and reflections in each chapter bring narrative strengths-based coaching to life. Filled with personal stories from her family and international coaching experiences, *Coaching A–Z* reads like an invitation to join Moon's world where there is always something 'else' to be added to the conversation to bring out the best of people and situations. This is a book for all coaches, educators, and parents who want, as Moon's father so often did, to turn trash into treasures. Read it and you will fall in love with words and the ways they can be used to generate delightfully positive and life-affirming possibilities."

DIANA WHITNEY, PhD, founder, Corporation for Positive Change; co-founder, Taos Institute; co-author, *The Power of Appreciative Inquiry*, *Appreciative Leadership*, and *Thriving Women, Thriving World*

"*Coaching A–Z* is a delightful and insightful guidebook for healing through conversation. Translating years of research and practice into simple, straightforward concepts, it shows how our words and questions can unleash strength, hope, and possibility in ourselves and others."

AMANDA TROSTEN-BLOOM, principal, Corporation for Positive Change; principal, Rocky Mountain Center for Positive Change; co-author, *Encyclopedia of Positive Questions*

"If you have ever had the opportunity to attend one of Haesun Moon's workshops or courses, you will recognize in this book her wonderful wit and wisdom woven into brilliant storytelling. She offers practical, and at the same time, powerful tools and concepts for us to use in our work whether in coaching, teaching, therapy, or in our daily lives, simply enriching our relationship with ourselves and each other. She brings to life ideas that will stay with me and reminds me of the beauty of orienting toward what we care about most deeply and recognizing and celebrating our progress!"

KRISTIN BODIFORD, PhD, principal, Community Strengths; adjunct professor, Dominican University; author

"Through the stories in this book—some of them moving, some of them very, very funny—a mindset emerges. This happens without the distraction caused by the fancy words that coaches and therapists usually use when they describe what they do. For the experienced practitioner, the book will be a reminder to stay humble, and for the beginner, it will be a learning experience. Interspersed without ever dominating are elegant tips and techniques that are useful for everyone doing this or similar kinds of work. You might cry at certain passages and you will surely laugh at others. I highly recommend this book for anyone interested in collaborative therapy and coaching."

HARRY KORMAN, MD, brief therapist, trainer, and supervisor; director, SIKT (Malmö); co-author, *More Than Miracles*

"Haesun Moon has delivered a brilliant breakthrough for anyone who works to help others create their 'preferred future.' After years of scholarship and practical experience, Moon boiled down the process of positive change into an elegant conversational model that has the best results of anything I've learned about or used in decades of executive coaching. Many people will live their best possible lives because of this very important process, so read this book and use it in your own life immediately!"

Coaching

Coaching

The Extraordinary Use of Ordinary Words

Haesun Moon PhD

Cataloguing in publication information
is available from Library and Archives Canada.
ISBN 978-1-77458-046-2 (paperback)
ISBN 978-1-77458-047-9 (ebook)

Page Two
pagetwo.com

Edited by Kendra Ward
Copyedited by Jenny Govier
Proofread by Alison Strobel
Cover and interior design by Jennifer Lum
Printed and bound in Canada by Friesens
Distributed in Canada by Raincoast Books
Distributed in the US and internationally by Macmillan

23 24 25 26   5 4 3 2

coachingatoz.com

For Dad.

Your story. Our story. And now my story.

I inconsolably miss you as I imagine

you holding this book.

—

For Mom.

You gave my heart a sight

and my mind a sound.

This is my gift for you

in profound gratitude and love.

Contents

A Gift of Better Conversation

DO YOU REMEMBER having a really good conversation? Who were you talking to? What were you talking about? What made it so good?

Some people just seem so naturally gifted in conversations; they make you feel understood, appreciated, or perhaps encouraged and valued. If every conversation did that, wouldn't that change your everyday whereabouts in your world?

The word "conversation" is an intriguing one. In mid-fourteenth-century Old French, the word *conversation* meant way of life. The way you show up in the world: your manners, actions, and habits. Its Latin root, *conversātiōnem*, offered another relevant meaning: where you habitually indwell. Your address, so to speak. Though these archaic meanings are obsolete in the word's use nowadays, we can still glimpse the intricate traces in its metaphorical use. For example, what stories do you live with? What stories frequently make your mind their abode? What occupies your heart-space? Habits of our heart give ears to the stories that enter our lives, and habits of our mind give voice to the stories we echo. Sometimes these stories hurt, sometimes they heal.

The practice of hosting healing conversations began probably well before the chronicles of the human race. In the recent century, some of them are documented in the form of talk therapy, literally "narrative" (from Latin, *narrare*) "cure" (from Greek, *therapeia*). The most common assumption embedded in talk therapy is that people's stories may lead to a cure. Whether people can find some faulty logic in their cognition or deeply rooted tales in their subconscious, talk therapy heavily relies on narration. How does talking actually cure? What kinds of talk lead to cure? These questions launched my decade-long quest as a communication scientist to research how coaching conversations work. After well over ten thousand hours of studying how conversations work, I realized something simple that completely changed my practice as a coach, as well as the pedagogy of the practice for me as an educator. The simple realization was this: *Not all narrative is curative!* Instead of blindly believing that *stories cure* (talk therapy), we ought to seek those *stories that cure* (therapeutic talk); we might even consider authoring curing narratives as we speak. Thought-twister, isn't it? So if that's the case, where are those stories held and how do we story them?

Ah, that's the magic, like *abracadabra*—"I create as I speak"! As two people converse, stories emerge and merge in the flow of shared meaning. Those stories happen in that in-between space as we sit with another, with many story bits to be told, to be heard, and to behold. We co-author and witness as stories are formed and transformed in our interactions, and we often wonder, *How did we get here?*

Now, that's perhaps where this book began for me. As I followed the meandering storylines of people in conversation, I noticed that some people repeatedly get off track, miss the exit, or even get lost in their own story-making. Yet some others almost effortlessly get back on track, find shortcuts, or even create their own path in the uncharted territory. What makes that difference?

This search birthed yet another very simple illustration: a listening compass. The compass has two lines, or axes, that cross in the middle: a horizontal timeline from past to future, and a vertical line that indicates positive content above the line and negative content below the line. When people tell their stories, they usually talk about either the past or the future (from left to right on the compass), and also about things they want either more of or less of in their life (from top to bottom).

Going counterclockwise from the top right corner, this leaves us with four sections, or quadrants:

1 The Preferred Future
2 The Resourceful Past
3 The Troubled Past
4 The Dreaded Future

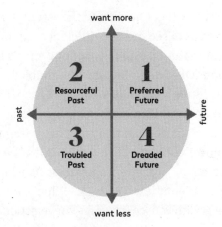

From Moon, H. (2020). Coaching: Using ordinary words in extraordinary ways. In S. McNamee, M.M. Gergen, C. Camargo-Borges & E.F. Rasera (Eds.), *The SAGE handbook of social constructionist practice* (pp. 246–257). SAGE Publications.

Where do you most frequently dwell in your stories? When the gravity of the troubled past (Quadrant 3) and the dreaded future (Quadrant 4) weigh you down, where's the closest exit? Is there a shortcut to the preferred future (Quadrant 1) and the resourceful past (Quadrant 2)? Where would you like to be?

By now, you may be wondering, *Is this a book about therapy or coaching or training?* And the quick answer is a big, smiley *Yes!* However you come to this conversation, I hold on to the assumption that people want to see positive differences in their life (Quadrant 1) and are already making efforts in that direction (Quadrant 2). Even the troubled past or dreaded future contribute to the clarity about what's wanted and what's already working in that direction. Some people call this compass a framework of healing. I've heard researchers call it a "heuristic of interaction." I've given it a serious name myself: Dialogic Orientation Quadrant. Whichever name resonates with you, consider it a conversational GPS as you and your fellow wayfinders—whether they be your colleagues or employees, your parents or your children, your clients or your students or your friends—master the craft of storying together.

And this mastery is not a mystery. Based on the thousands of hours of research that earned me a doctorate degree, I can tell you that storying together may begin with simply using our ordinary words in extraordinary ways. *It could be as easy as ABC!* is the exuberant hope behind this book—that you will begin conversing with yourself and others differently as a result. I've also written this book mindful of those of you who might be in the middle of running the race of life, so you can take a brief pit stop. It's also for those who might be in between lives, so you can take an extended sabbatical. For that reason, I've included a Reflection Guide at the end of each chapter with which you can simply pause and rest. This book is my heart-deep invitation for you to imagine the stories, remember the lessons, and experiment with the reflections to change your own conversations—where your life dwells.

With love,
Haesun Moon
Toronto

Already

Focus on the efforts a person has made in the desired direction, rather than on next steps.

HAS ANYONE EVER told you you're almost there, to just push a little harder? A few years ago, I was recovering from a car accident. I worked with different therapists and trainers who helped me with rebuilding muscles. Watching them work was fascinating, as they had different tactics to motivate even a reluctant client like me.

"C'mon, you're almost there, gimme just three more!" said Tommy the Trainer, who seemed so talented at... sweating.

"If you don't exercise, you'll lose those muscles eventually," said Theo the Therapist, who had a knack for... scaring.

I also met occasional guilt-trippers who told me that my recovery would have been quicker had I been more active before the accident. That helps, right?

Then one day, a petite young trainer walked into my life.

"Hi, I'm Diane."

"Hey... what are we working on today?" I asked, already feeling tired. The regular thirty-minute routine consisted of five exercises with three repetitions (two, if I complained hard enough).

"Well, what have you been working on so far?"

"My legs? Lower back?"

"For what?" she asked, making notes.

"Strengthening, I think? Balancing too," I said, puzzled because these things already should have been in my file. Why was she asking? Was she new at this?

"Strength and balance... hmm. When and where do you notice strength and balance now?"

Okay, that was new. I hadn't been asked that before. Other trainers usually asked me when I felt weakest and most unbalanced and how that negatively affected my life.

"Well... when I'm teaching, and I do feel strong enough now to work eight hours straight. I don't feel tired or even achy."

"You must like what you do," she said, looking up from her notes and smiling.

> What moves people is not necessarily detailing *how* they will reach what they want. Motivation starts, almost always, with discovering *why* they want to reach that.

"Sounds like it, huh?" I said, smiling back.

"So, you already know that becoming stronger and more balanced is important for you to continue doing what you love... and it sounds like you've already recovered enough to be able to work like that. Now, what have you done so far to get as strong and balanced as this?"

The heart of the conversation

At the heart of every coaching conversation resides an inquiry about what people want. Some say they want more or less of the same, while others want something or someone to change. How do you respond when people tell you what they want? You might explore the want. We call people's wants "goals," "outcomes," "objectives," or other similar words indicating some endpoint or destination. You may even go further to determine how they might get there. We call this an "action plan," "strategies," "next steps," or similar words that describe the means to the endpoint. You have undoubtedly participated in this type of conversation more than once to lay out a plan full of efforts now to be made.

In my experience, what moves people is not necessarily detailing *how* they will reach what they want. Motivation starts, almost always, with discovering *why* they want to reach that. Determining the "why" of the what ("I'm exercising so that I have more stamina for doing what I love") naturally drives the "how" of the what ("You'll need to do three reps of five exercises"). The delight continues as they discover how much they have already moved in their preferred direction ("What have you done so far to get as strong and balanced as this?"). The role of a good coach, guide, and listener in any dialogue is not to cheerlead the conversation partners with you're-almost-there messages, but simply to invite them to remember what they're *already doing* to move in that direction.

Reflection Guide

Reflect, for a moment, on a sense of purpose and progress that you have experienced. This may have been because of an important decision, a surprising risk, or even a familiar struggle you've worked through.

- How did it help you to discover what's really important to you?

- What did it tell you about what you care about?

- What's already clear about why you care about what you care about?

Becoming

Orient people's attention to what is wanted,
acknowledging what is needed and believing that
they already have what it takes.

DO YOU REMEMBER being asked when you were little, "Who do you want to be when you grow up?"

"Nightingale!" was the first answer from one girl in my class. "Dr. Schweitzer!" was also a popular answer. The exclamations continued and included everything from teacher to police officer to scientist. I was just three or four when my parents first asked me this big question.

"I want to be King Arthur!" is what they got.

I don't recall their exact faces, but I can imagine my young parents exchanging somewhat puzzled looks. I do remember what my mom did after that.

"Dear King, come get your lunch," she'd call out.

"King Haesun, can you please put your dish in the sink?" she'd ask.

The radical acceptance
of believing in the other's
becoming is the very glue that
mends and bonds many
relations we hold near.

She diligently addressed me as I wanted, as if she believed I could be whatever I wanted to be. And I took on many new titles after that: Astronaut Moon, Detective Haesun, Journalist Miss Moon, my moniker changing with my dreams. As I got older, I grew out of some dreams and some dreams grew out of me. One day, when I thought I had long moved away from the question, my little nephew reignited it.

"Auntie, who did you want to be when you grow up?"

My dad looked up from his sushi dish and Mom arched her eyebrows.

"I always wanted to be..." I momentarily paused and looked away as so many thoughts and faces whipped by my mind's eye. I returned my gaze to meet his. "I always wanted to be who I have become now."

"Oh, cool," he said nonchalantly with another bite of his dinner, never realizing the weightiness of his question. For that, I gave him another big scoop of steamed vegetables.

"Now, finish your veggies, Spider-Man."

As our chatter continued, I saw my parents exchange warm smiles across the table.

Radically accept another's truth

When I was first learning to coach, I asked many teachers and mentors what we ought to do as coaches in conversation with our clients. Some said, "Ask good questions." Others said, "Be an empathic listener." One of the most memorable responses came from my mentor and one of the founders of Solution-Focused practices, Peter De Jong, who simply asked, "Do you believe your clients?"

When working with a client who believed that her upstairs neighbor beamed shockwaves down through her ceiling, Steve de Shazer, a pioneer of Solution-Focused brief therapy, simply believed her. He paid attention to her life logic, her way of making sense of her world, instead of being preoccupied with judging whether her story was true. In her logic, the neighbor's shockwave was the reason she could not sleep well. So, the conversation turned to what might help her get a better night's sleep in a way that made sense to her. Another radical story comes from Insoo Kim Berg, also a key founder of Solution-Focused practices, when she responded to a client who said it would take a miracle for her life to be better. That was the client's logic as she coped with life and hoped that all her difficulties would disappear. Whether Insoo herself believed in miracles was irrelevant. Believing her client, Insoo asked what this miracle would do for her. This interaction between Insoo and her client became an iconic moment, giving birth to what's been dubbed "The Miracle Question," now widely adopted in mainstream therapy and coaching as an intervention to explore the client's preferred future, their hopes and dreams.

As you sit with others in conversation, how do you respond to their hopes and dreams? As they share their preferred ways of doing their life, do your habitual assumptions get in the way of believing that they are already well on their way? As they dream themselves into existence, in what ways do you witness and acknowledge their becoming? This "radical acceptance" of believing in the other's becoming is not just a tool for professional coaches; it's the very glue that mends and bonds many relations we hold near.

Reflection Guide

As you reflect on how far you have traveled on your own path of becoming who you are today, you may recall others who believed in you along the way.

- What characteristics, interests, and passions showed up early in your life that signaled your becoming who you are today?

- What are some of your small and big dreams that came true? Who believed you or believed in you? What difference did it make having someone believe in you?

Now, let's experiment with this idea in conversation:

- Ask someone (a client, family member, friend, colleague, and so on) *what's becoming clearer* in their life as they go through some life crisis. As you listen, pay attention to what they say is becoming clearer, and focus less on the content of their life crisis.

Care

Be curious about what matters to another person
instead of what is the matter with the person.

THIS COMMUTE WASN'T different from my usual early morning drive to work. Even the bottleneck at the entrance to the hospital where I worked was the same. The overnight snowfall wasn't helping, but the weather wasn't bad enough to altogether halt the flow of traffic. But my friend Angela was driving me that day, and we were a lot quieter in the car than usual. Waiting to turn into the hospital driveway, Angela briefly looked over at me. "You're gonna be okay. I'll be praying for you."

Oh, that's right. Her remarks reminded me that I was at the hospital today not as a staff member, but as a patient.

"Just drop me off at the corner and go home. I'll call you when I'm out," I said, smiling.

"Nope," she said, shaking her head. "I'm coming in with you."

We walked together to the surgery registration desk. I handed over my picture ID and watched my hand quiver. "Name, birthday, address?" The clerk confirmed my identity with three simple questions and pointed to the back of the waiting room. "The changeroom is over there." I stripped off my hefty winter clothes and crammed them full into a drawstring plastic bag. The blue hospital gown hung flimsy and I felt overly exposed, even when I tied all the strings as snug as I could. An attending nurse found me peeking sheepishly out of the changeroom, and she escorted me to a room with a gurney. Angela followed closely behind, and we waited as the nurse looped my wrist with a fluorescent yellow patient ID and put an IV in my arm. Angela had more questions for the nurse than I did, and I found it strangely comforting to feel taken care of. Someone else arrived, a porter. Angela took my fidgeting hand in hers and looked right at me before the porter began to wheel me out of the room.

"You'll be fine. I'll be there when you wake up."

As we moved out into the hallway and toward the operating room, the porter looked down at me with a big pearly smile.

"I'm Jerome. First-time surgery?" he asked in a voice deep like that of a sports broadcaster.

"Yeah. Very first time," I said, smiling back at him.

"They have good doctors here," he said, nodding as we turned a corner. "You're in good hands." Before I could respond, he added, "We're going to the OR floor. Enjoy the ride."

Then, as I was wheeled through familiar parts of the hospital, I noticed something sweet: the ceiling tiles. Every other one along our route to the OR was painted with images and messages. My eyes quickly tracked the passing tiles as Jerome turned several more times before finally coming to a stop.

"Here we are, Miss Moon. I'll pick you up when you're done."

"Jerome, you will be the one picking me up?" I asked, sitting up halfway as he walked away.

"Yes," he said, looking back with another big grin. "But you won't know that because you'll be sleeping. Good luck."

Jerome left me in the hallway outside the OR. It was much quieter than I would have thought. I was the only person there. I looked out the window to my right and saw the wing that housed my office.

My mind wandered. As I lay back down, I heard a door open on my left. Three people emerged dressed exactly the same: yellow gown, head cap, and mask. My heart fluttered. One person lowered their mask and said, "Hey, Haesun, you ready?" I sat up and scanned as quickly as I could to figure out who it was and realized it was my surgeon.

"Oh my goodness, Grace, it's you. You look so different in that."

"Better or worse?" she asked, chuckling, before she introduced me to the team one by one. "Now, come on in," Grace said, gesturing like she was inviting me into her living room.

She helped me up from the gurney and we entered the OR together. It was completely different from what I expected—well lit, with yellow-painted walls, a small metal bed in the middle of the room; definitely not as cold as what you see on the TV shows. As the team busily set up, Grace asked me to first sit, then lie on the metal bed, the operating table.

"The table might be a bit cold. But we have a warm pillow for you," she said.

Maybe I was a bit too rigid or slow, because Grace came over and sat right next to me.

"Hey, you okay?"

"

If you are curious about *what matters* to them, you are inviting them on a quest to discover what they care about, what truly matters, and what makes their heart sing.

My eyes were welling up for some reason, and Grace reached out to touch my clenched fist.

"I'm here, Haesun. I'll be here the whole time. Don't you worry."

The first thing I remembered when I woke up from that surgery was the final moment in the OR, when Grace was holding my hand in hers while holding a gas mask over my face with her other hand, looking straight at me with what I can only call *love*.

Curating stories beyond simple narrating

People often ask how I define coaching. "Curating stories of purpose, possibilities, and progress," is my answer.

The word "curate" comes from the Latin noun *cura*, meaning care. Indeed, the act of selecting, organizing, and presenting the stories we care about is an active choice to take care of ourselves and others. No wonder the same root word is shared with the word "cure," as some of us may describe conversation as a healing experience for a heart inflicted with unwelcome stories and inherited narratives. And such a conversation becomes available when

the listener is present with their full "curiosity"—
another word that bears the word *cura* at its heart.

Imagine a conversation in which you help someone curate a story of purpose, possibility, and progress
for themselves:

> AJ: So, I'm stuck with that negative thought pat-
> tern right now. That old record keeps playing in
> the background, some days so much louder than
> other days.

> Coach: Oh, okay. Tell me more about that.

> AJ: The negative thought patterns keep saying
> that—

> Coach: No, I mean, you said there are some days
> when it's louder and—

> AJ: Yes, definitely, like yesterday.

> Coach: So, you have some days when it's not as
> loud as yesterday.

> AJ: Yeah, for sure.

> Coach: Well, tell me more about those days when
> it's much quieter than other days.

AJ: Um... it usually happens when I have my friends over, I guess. Or I have an urgent project that I need to work on.

Coach: So, when you have your friends over or when you work on a project, the old record gets quiet.

AJ: Yes, exactly. Because I am occupied. Especially with my friends; they know me so well and I don't have to pretend to be someone else.

Coach: Ah... and that helps.

What you are curious about will orient your conversation partner's attention accordingly. If you are curious about *what's the matter*, you set them on a path with your questions to look closely into what's wrong, what's not working, and what might be getting in their way. If you are curious about *what matters* to them, you are inviting them on a quest to discover what they care about, what truly matters, and what makes their heart sing.

Reflection Guide

You may feel that some people in your life "get you" and maybe you "get them." Think of those moments and interactions when you felt both connected and understood in a meaningful way.

- What do they "get" about you that is meaningful for you?

- In your interactions with them, how do you experience their care? How do they experience your care?

It is often said that what you care about will show up in your schedule book and your bank book.

- What might your current calendar tell you about what you are spending your time on?

- Suppose you designed your calendar around what you care about. What would be different about your schedule?

- When was the last time you had a day with an intentional schedule of doing what you care most about?

Difference

Activate a person's wishes for
positive change in their future and accentuate
positive experiences in their past.

A T AN EARLY MORNING training session that I was attending, the facilitator suggested that the group respond to an icebreaker question. I wasn't particularly fond of it: "If you won the lottery, would you quit working?" *Oh dear*, I thought, somewhat unimpressed, and turned my chair to my partner to pose this question.

"So, would you?" my partner asked first, sounding and looking a bit too chirpy for so early in the morning.

"Nope," I said. "What about you?" I leaned back and took a sip of coffee.

"I think I would."

"Well, that's a surprise," I remarked, sounding more skeptical than surprised.

"How so?"

"You look like you like your job," I observed.

"Well, I do," she said. Then she added, sotto voce, gazing out the window, "But I have something else I want to do more."

In the ensuing minutes I learned a lot about my partner. Her name was Chris. She would buy a big piece of land with her lottery win. That land would give her enough space to build a campground.

"Oh, and a farm with horses and rescue dogs, maybe cows," she added, gazing out the window again. The campground with many cabins would host summer camps, retreats, even conferences or schools. The farm would hire employees.

"And," she said, returning her gaze to me, "we'd be able to have children with developmental disabilities and their families come there and spend time together."

My head nodded and then my heart registered what she had just said. And so, I uttered my go-to question: "Okay. And why is this so important to you?"

Her glasses glinted in the morning light as she considered the question.

"For the kids, I want them to just ... be. Be there. Be themselves. And for the families, a little rest goes a long way."

"A little rest for the family, and for the kids to just be, just be there."

"Yeah."

"That's something important to them?"

"Oh, yes. That really will make all the difference."

"What difference will it make?"

"For the kids, they will know that they belong."

"Belong. Okay."

"Yeah, and the families, they will know that they are not alone."

"Wow."

"And the kids will contribute and participate."

"It sounds like you've thought about this a lot."

"Oh, yes."

"And it's something you really care about. What difference would this make for you?"

Our ten minutes had now quickly passed. The facilitator began rallying us to shift our chairs and face the front of the room again.

"I'd know that Robin will be proud of me," Chris almost whispered.

"Who's Robin?"

"My sister. It will be in memory of Robin," she said, smiling.

Coaching is not just questioning differently; it's more listening differently.

Follow the trail

You might wonder how my conversation with Chris moved from an icebreaker about winning the lottery to a heartwarming dream of commemorating her sister, Robin. Her wishes seemed to take a little detour. From lottery to land. From farm to family. From the kids' cabin to Chris's Robin. Maybe it wasn't a detour after all; maybe it was a shortcut to what she truly cares about. How did we get there? I simply followed the trail of some positive differences that she initially said she wanted—like winning the lottery and quitting her job. And then I tracked the differences those would make—like buying some land and building a campground. At the end of my conversation with Chris, what did she seem to truly care about? Not winning the lottery but minding the memory of her sister.

People often speak about what they want to see change in their lives. *What if I had a different family? A different job? What if I chose something different?* Even outside a treatment room, an office, or a classroom, how many times do we daydream about different possibilities and scenarios, only to wake up to our reality feeling less than fulfilled?

One of a few significant lessons I have learned from coaching is *listening differently*. When you listen to people daydream, what if you believe their daydreams and ask them about those dreams? Might that lead to positive differences, the way Chris led to Robin? Based on what your conversation partner says they want to be different, you can follow the trail by asking more about the very difference those small differences might make, for example:

- Suppose your family somehow changed. What difference would that make for you?

- Suppose you could design your own dream job. What would that job offer you?

- Suppose you made a different choice. What might that do for you?

You might be surprised to see how quickly people get to what they truly care about, just by your listening differently. Listen to that trail of many small but significant differences and respond to those special paths they've taken in search of their meaning.

Reflection Guide

Here's a quick conversation you can host with yourself:

- In what areas of your life would you like to see a positive difference?

- Suppose that positive difference somehow comes true. What other differences would it make?

- What difference would those other differences make for you and other people specifically? Why is that important or meaningful for you?

Else

Invite other perspectives and available resources a person may have not yet considered or considered relevant.

WHEN MY NEPHEW Jeremy was in grade two, I had to drop off his winter boots at his school one day. As I approached his classroom, I heard the teacher's voice through the propped-open door.

"So, how do you get to nine from three?"

Math was not my favorite subject growing up. Maybe it's the way it was taught to me. Maybe it's because there were a lot of irrelevant problems to solve and so many formulae to remember. There were no stories to math, no room for creativity; answers were either right or wrong. So, when I heard the teacher say what she did, I thought, *What an endearing way to teach addition.*

"Yes, Jeremy," the teacher called out. My nephew must have put up his hand. Good for him!

"Add four," I heard him say confidently.

Attaboy!

But hold on. Add four? That makes it seven, not nine! Wrong answer, buddy. I waited, expecting the teacher to correct him.

"Okay, and what else?" the teacher asked.

Wait. What? What did she mean, "What else"?

"What else do we need to do to get to nine? So far, we have three plus four."

I heard the sound of chalk tapping on the board.

"Add three!" another small voice blurted out.

Oh dear. Still wrong. I lightly shook my head.

"Oopsy-daisy, we just went over the nine!"

I heard giggling over the sound of chalk gliding.

"What else do we need?" the teacher pushed.

"Subtract one!" and "Minus one!" came the replies.

"Voilà! We're there!" the teacher exclaimed gleefully.

"Yay!" the children shouted in unison.

"Well done, everyone! Wanna do one more?"

Unbelievably, they said yes.

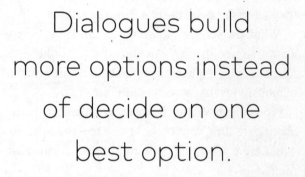

Dialogues build
more options instead
of decide on one
best option.

Move from either–or to both–and

I meet many people searching for the one right answer: tired parents second-guessing their parenting choices, senior leaders doubting their operational decisions, people in transition searching for meaningful work. "I just hope I'm doing the right thing," they often say as we begin our conversations.

What do you say to someone looking for an answer to be either right or wrong? Life would be so much simpler if questions could be answered unambiguously, just like that, wouldn't it?

"You must have a good reason to make that choice about parenting your child," I said to a tired parent. "What are you hoping your child might learn from this?"

The almost teary parent told me they wanted their child to learn the life lesson that choices always carry consequences. "I know they hate me for it now, but they will thank me one day," she muttered through her sighs.

"It's not easy making decisions that impact others' lives," I remarked to a doubtful leader. "What else tells you that you're moving in the right direction?"

This leader responded with conviction that he was proud to have so far chosen scenarios that favor people over profit. "But not everyone knows about it or agrees with it," he shrugged.

"Who else knows and appreciates your heart for people?" I asked.

A pause. A weighty one. "My closest circle. It means so much to me that they trust me and stand right by me." He smiled pensively. "That's what matters to me. I guess I am doing okay after all."

"You must have experienced that special feeling when you're doing something meaningful," I said to a young job seeker. "When else have you felt it?" They told me they felt it when they were contributing to something bigger than themselves.

What warms my heart is that, although their lives track different stories, all three clients arrived at the same place by the end of our conversations: "I guess I'm already on the right track."

Reflection Guide

Here's a set of curiosities and activities that invite you to consider various perspectives.

- Think about a small decision that, after you made it, turned out to be a great decision. What did you learn from that experience?

- What is a memorable story you have about yourself? What other interpretations of it might be available?

- Suppose you met your younger self from that memory. What words of wisdom and encouragement would you offer?

First

Positively trigger people to pay close
attention to small but significant turning points—
from familiar and unwanted patterns toward
unfamiliar yet wanted patterns.

BEING THE YOUNGEST of three children in the family means I learned a lot second-hand, really before it was my turn to learn. Learning to speak, learning to count, learning to read and write—I picked up a lot of things at an earlier age than did my siblings, as I learned through them vicariously. My mom was delighted to see me grasping things ahead of schedule. Her delight lasted probably until I started studying how to be a teenager before I was a teen. I stomped around the house for no reason. I thumped up the music on my headphones, and I answered most questions posed by adults with "I don't know" or (even cooler) "Whatever" from deep beneath my draping hoodie. Sound familiar?

One irritated day, I decided to practice the challenge-your-mom-for-no-reason skill. I walked into the kitchen where she was getting dinner ready, pretending to get a glass of water.

"Oh, hello. You hungry?" she asked with a smile.

I shrugged my shoulders before asking something obvious. "Mom, I'm your youngest of three, right?"

"Yes, love, it's very possible that's so," she joked.

"Then, you already had two other kids to practice parenting with, right?"

"That's an interesting way to see it," she said, pondering.

That's when I shot out the line I had prepared for her. "Then how come you didn't parent me better? You should've done a better job."

Mom looked at me a bit surprised.

"Yes, good point," she said, tilting her head, "but it was my first time raising you, and I'm still getting to know you, as you are becoming more you every day."

Her smile grew bigger as I stood there. I hadn't seen that coming. That was awkward. I shrugged my shoulders and turned around. As I prepared to stomp back to my room, I noticed that my legs had lost their steam and I was standing a bit taller. I felt Mom's warm gaze follow me all the way down the hall until I closed the door behind me.

Suppose, rather than impose, the signs that spell hope

We remember our many firsts: first date, first car, first job. Many parents wait in exuberant anticipation for their child to mumble their first word, then wobble their first steps. Yet, soon enough, children seem to talk too much and run too fast. The delight of the first fades all too soon. Some of my most rewarding moments happen when I work with families experiencing those dwindling delights. Each family member is ready to tell stories of the others being tyrants, micromanagers, or disrespectful.

"It's his way or the highway!" the disrespectful child complains.

"They don't listen to anyone!" the tyrant father counters.

When families, teams, or groups get stuck in a tug of war like this, I ask them, "What will be the first sign that will indicate things are getting better, even a little bit?"

"He'll listen to what I have to say before he starts going off," the daughter declares. The father sighs and shakes his head.

"And suppose he does that, he listens to what you have to say. What difference will that make for you?"

"

We look for
evidence that
supports our beliefs
about who we are,
who they are,
what they do, and
what we do.

"

"Then . . . it will be like . . . I can trust him again," she says, looking up to see him frowning slightly.

"And when you trust him again, what first few things will you start doing again?"

There's a long pause, as if they're both holding their breath.

"I might start asking him for advice, actually."

The father's expression changes to slight surprise, and the two exchange brief gazes.

The well-known confirmation bias plays against us many times. We look for evidence that supports our beliefs—in this case, the labels we have for others. More tyranny shows up from the tyrant father, more insolence comes from the disrespectful kid. We spool our threads of biased evidence to weave narratives about who we are, who they are, what they do, and what we do.

When you ask about the first sign or the first few things, as I did with this family, it's often like pulling the initial thread that begins to unravel a tapestry they have woven. At work, a manager might ask an employee, "What are the first few things that will signal your relationship with your team member is getting better?" At school, a teacher might ask a student, "What could be the first sign that you're getting better at this subject?" At a hospital, a health-care professional might ask a patient in recovery, "What was, or what will be, the first sign of your healing?"

When asked such questions, people begin to see things they didn't before. They start to see things they want to see. The word "first" invites people to re-look at their familiar interactions differently. The act of re-looking in English literally spells "respect": *re-* (again) + *spect* (look). Isn't that fascinating?

Reflection Guide

Different situations offer us different opportunities to reflect on what we've learned and what we hope for. Especially as we consider a troubled past or a dreaded future, we can re-look at the situation from more useful perspectives.

- Thinking back on a situation you found challenging, what was the first sign that things were getting better? What did you notice about yourself that told you that you were coping better?

- Thinking ahead to a situation that might challenge you soon, what will be the first few things you notice about yourself that will tell you you're moving in the right direction?

Good

(Enough)

Value people's own measure of
what makes their life worth living.

THE TASK SOUNDED deceptively straight-forward. Bathe a two-year-old. I was left in charge of my two nephews, and it was time for Nathan's bath. I'd seen it done but I'd never done it myself. How hard could it be?

"Time for a bath," I announced.

"Yay!" the boys cheered, running down the hall-way of the apartment to the bathroom. Nathan grabbed his rubber ducky, Jeremy his Disney towel.

"Excuse me, boys," I said as I weaved past them and into the tiny space.

A mirrored medicine cabinet hung above the vanity, with fingerprints at the bottom right cor-ner of the glass, evidence of frequent opening. The toilet crouched low and tight between the tub and sink. The tub showed faint water stains from a drip-ping spout below round hot and cold faucet knobs marked with red and blue dots. From the red one, a stopper dangled on a beaded chain.

"Okay, let's get some water first," I said as I plugged the drain with the stopper.

"Okay," five-year-old Jeremy said.

"Okie," two-year-old Nathan mimicked, holding his rubber ducky and ready for a swim.

The red knob squeaked when I turned it, and water began gushing out. I turned the blue knob but was unsure if it added much to the waterfall. As the three of us stood watching, I began to wonder if the water might be too hot or too cold.

"I need to measure the water," I concluded aloud and began looking for a thermometer.

"What are you looking for?" Jeremy asked as I fumbled through the vanity cabinet.

"Something to measure the water with," I said, looking inside the medicine cabinet.

"Oh, I know where it is," Jeremy said, running out of the bathroom.

Nathan looked at me and shrugged. I ruffled his hair. Clanking in the kitchen was muffled by the water spurting in the tub. Following a brief moment of silence, Jeremy ran back into the crowded bathroom.

"Here it is," he said, proudly handing his rookie auntie a yellow retractable tape measure.

"Oh," I said, my mouth slightly agape as I took the heavy-duty tape measure from his hand. I looked over at Nathan, who blinked twice.

"All right, let's measure it," I said, turning around to the tub, where my glasses quickly fogged up from the steam. "Go get a pencil and paper," I told Jeremy as I shut off both knobs.

"Okay!" he said as he scurried out and Nathan wobbled behind him.

"Walk, don't run," I cautioned them.

Jeremy pitter-pattered back with a notepad and a pen. Nathan followed right behind with his rubber ducky. Jeremy clicked the top of the pen, ready to write. I drew out the metal tape and measured the tub.

"Forty-five inches for length," I called out.

"Four... tee... five," Jeremy drawled, printing on the notepad while I shifted to measure the width.

"Thirty inches wide."

"Thir... tee," Jeremy repeated as Nathan climbed onto the toilet lid.

I stooped to reach the floor, and Nathan leaned on my shoulder with one arm as he perched on the toilet.

Asking, "How did you get here?" unfolds the logic of doing one's life. We simply listen to what they want, what's important to them, and what they care about.

"And twenty inches for the height."

"Twen..." As Jeremy was about to write it down, I stood with a slight grunt and let the tape measure whir back into its coil. He looked up.

"Jeremy, this doesn't give me the information I need."

"Oh?" He looked puzzled. "What do you mean?"

"Well, I need to measure the temperature. I don't know if the water is too hot or too cold for Nathan." I didn't want to miss a teaching moment. "How do we measure the temperature, Jeremy?"

"Oh," he said, looking at his brother. "That's easy. Ask him. It's his bath." Nathan tugged at my sleeve, and I turned to see him throw his rubber ducky in the water.

"Wait," he said, still holding my sleeve. After a minute, he reached with his free arm to retrieve the ducky. He checked the bottom and held it up for me to see.

"It's good 'nuff."

I stood there dumbfounded by the temperature-sensitive ducky with the indicator on its bottom as Nathan hopped in the tub, reassuring me with a thumbs-up and a nod.

Ask, "How did you get here?" more often than, "How will you get there?"

When people work on something, they often want to do more and be better. Parents want to do more for their children and be better at parenting. Managers want to encourage their teams to produce more (quantity) and better (quality) results at work. Students want to do better (probably not more) at school, right?

"I want to be the best I can be," a young manager said.

"Okay. On a scale of ten to one, where ten is the best that you can imagine being and one is the opposite, where are you today?" I asked.

"Oh, like... at a six today," she responded.

Now what? What would you say to that?

With or without any prompt, people often continue to explain why they are not at ten but only at six, or any other number below ten they chose, for that matter. They lack something—this is a *deficit frame*. They may persist to plan out what they need to do to get to that perfect score of ten because they feel that any number below ten is not good enough. What if you interrupt that thought?

"Ah, you are at six already. How did you manage to get up to six?" I asked.

"Well, I think I've made some progress since we last talked." The manager continued on to talk about why she was already at a six, not one or two or even five. She had something—this is a *resource frame*.

Once people have a resource frame, reminding themselves of their progress, they may indicate someone or something that enabled their progress. Scale is a metaphor of existing progress, after all. The interest is in *how they already got here* rather than *how they will get higher* on the scale.

Now what? Where do you go from here as your conversation partner speaks about their resources and progress? Often the temptation is to jump into getting people closer to the perfect ten. But, if you do that, you assume that where they are at today may not be *good enough*. Instead, you can ask:

"So, where would be a good enough place for you on this scale?"

"Well . . . it would be nice if I can be at six and a half by next week."

"A half-point higher."

"Yeah. It's a small step forward."

"And what would you notice that's good enough about you at that point?"

And the conversation continues as they describe what's good enough a half-point up rather than how they're going to get there. And so, they unfold their logic of doing their life, and you just listen—to what they want, what's important to them, and what they care about.

Reflection Guide

Think of an area of your life that you'd like to examine. It might be work, relationships, habits, choices, interactions, and so on.

- On a scale of ten to one, where ten is *I feel that I am at my best in that area* and one is the opposite, where would you say you are today?

- What got you to that number already; what or who helped? How did you contribute to that number in a positive way?

- Where would be a good enough point on that scale for you within the next four to six weeks?

- What is different or better about yourself when you are at that "good enough" point?

Hope

Create a tangible possibility and a sense
of agency through a detailed description of
the other's preferred future.

IT WAS A beautiful Saturday morning when the phone rang from an unknown number and I reluctantly picked up.

"Hello...?"

"Oh, what a beautiful day. Good morning there," the caller said.

"Good morning. Who is this?" I asked, slightly annoyed since he hadn't identified himself.

"My name is Joe and I'm calling from—" I forget the company he worked for, but it was clearly a sales call.

"I'm sorry, but I'm not interested in buying anything," I said, ready to hang up.

"No, I'm not selling anything. I just want you to consider three questions I'm about to ask," he said, sounding rather convincing. "It may change your life."

"All right, let's hear it." I was genuinely intrigued by this telemarketer posing life-changing questions.

"Okay, first question. Don't you wanna have more time to spend on what you really wanna do with your life?"

What an absurd question.

"I already do," I replied, my eyeroll unseen by him.

"You do? Okay. Well, then, the second question. Don't you want to make more money?" he asked rather confidently.

"Uh, no. I make enough money. I don't need more," I replied.

"Oh, you do? Hmm, interesting. People usually say yes to that," he almost mumbled to himself. "Okay, the last question. Um, do you want to be happier?"

Now, theoretically, I know that the answer is supposed to be yes. Who would say no? But the very question feels somewhat unfair, given that the whole world pushes the narrative that we need to be happy.

"Actually, Joe, I'm so content with my life right now," I said, emphasizing each of my words. It felt rude to just hang up, so I hung on.

There was a pause before he cleared his throat.

"Um . . . may I ask what you do?" His voice toned down a bit. "You said you live your life doing what you love, making enough money from it, and you can't be happier."

"I guess I did," I said, smiling. "I work with people to help them figure out what they really want. I see a lot of positive changes in their relationships at home and at work. Now, Joe, do you have an area in your life where you hope to see some positive changes?"

"Yes, I absolutely do."

"Would you like to know more about how you can have better conversations about that?"

"Yes. Where do I sign up?"

With a chuckle, I told him how he could check out the coaching program at the university.

Three months later, I was facilitating an open house for the program. We had a huge gathering that evening. After we finished the official program and Q&A, I was packing up my bag at the front of the room when I noticed a young man in a gray suit walking toward me. He had a big grin on his face and reached out his hand to introduce himself. "Hi," he said, "remember me?" You guessed it. That was Joe.

Keep on keeping on

When I ask my clients what they hope to see that's different or better as a result of coming to see me, they often respond with, "To be happier." The pursuit of happiness in its many forms is a popular topic. People say they'd be happier if they became richer, smarter, healthier, taller, thinner, thicker, older, or younger. (Yes, some actually say younger.) This if–then logic of the pursuit of happiness isn't surprising if you look closely at the root word of "happy": *hap* (noun), meaning chance or fortune. This fascinating root is found in other words like *hap*pening, *hap*hazard, and *hap*penstance—in other words, occurrences beyond your control.

I learned the difference between hope and happiness in a conversation with Gina, a young patient with a terminal illness who was considering medical assistance in dying.[1] When I asked her what she hoped for that was different or better as a result of having a conversation with me, she said, "I hope to finish well." She shared her fears and worries about leaving her two small children behind. I asked her what she considered would end by dying.

---

[1] In Canada, it became legal in June 2016 for eligible adults to request medical assistance in dying.

Words, like living fossils, carry certain impressions of the past and create new impressions as we use them. How do you spell hope with your words?

"Pain. Being a burden."

Then I asked how she might know she was finishing well. She talked about her wish to die with dignity and leave a legacy of love for her family. "I want my boys to know that they are deeply loved," she said with a teary smile. I had barely anything left to say following that weighty statement. By the end of our conversation, she had her hand on my shoulder. "I know it's not a happy ending. But I'm now dying with hope," she said. Two weeks later, she passed away the way she chose, surrounded by loved ones.

Her voice still echoes—*I'm now dying with hope*—and this perhaps was only a glimpse. What does it possibly mean to hold on to hope while you are breathing your last breath? How is that hope made?

After this experience, I began describing my coaching work in health care as a "language of hope." It might be more precise to call it "*languaging* hope." This implies an intentional and attentional choice to craft hope where happiness may or may not fit. Words, like living fossils, carry certain impressions of the past and create new impressions as we use them. Unless we *language* hope with our words, we may soon languish. How do you spell hope with your words?

Reflection Guide

Life can be surprising as it unfolds. You may find yourself feeling surrounded in an unexpected situation, whispering to yourself, "I can't believe this is happening to me." Reflect on a moment like this that you have experienced.

- What were some significant discoveries from that experience about what you deeply value?

- What helped you to *keep on keeping on* in that situation?

- Suppose you could go back in time to talk to yourself in that moment. What might you say?

Special note to the reader who may be going through a particularly difficult time in life right now:

- What are some small habits that you do on a daily basis? (For example, stretching, walking, making a cup of tea or coffee, using the same mug or cup, writing, or putting on indoor shoes.)

- Choose up to five small habits that you'd like to keep. For each habit, please complete this sentence: "This habit helps me to..." Feel free to update the sentence over time.

- Pay attention to how many times you catch yourself in your habit throughout the day.

Instead

Pivot from "what's not wanted" stories by
asking about "what's wanted" in its place.

LINING UP AT a grocery store makes me slightly antsy. Growing up, my mom took me grocery shopping, and I happily tagged along because the always-packed market was full of vibrant sights, sounds, and smells. Every now and then I got a surprise goody to munch on. She told me I was a big help because I diligently checked expiry dates on milk cartons and meticulously examined every egg for cracks. She taught me how to choose the sweetest watermelon just by tapping, and occasionally I was allowed to choose the kind of meat we'd have for dinner.

One day, when I was nine years old, we rolled our full shopping cart through the crowded aisles to the cashier who seemed to have the shortest line. "I think she works very fast," Mom surmised. A long line quickly formed behind us, inching in on us, though the line in front wasn't moving. Finally, the customer paid the cashier and the line moved forward a little.

"Next!" the cashier called out, and the next customer began placing their groceries on the counter.

"Oh, I forgot something. Can you just stay here with the cart?" Mom said more than asked. "I'll be right back," she added before disappearing into the crowd. That's when I noticed that the cashier seemed to be working faster than before. Suddenly, the line in front of me was getting shorter and shorter, while the line behind got longer and longer.

"Next!" The cashier beckoned.

The man ahead of me started placing his items on the counter, and the cashier swiftly rang them through. I felt my chest getting stuffier and I rubbernecked to look for Mom, who was nowhere to be seen. The gentleman reached for his wallet as the cashier bagged his last item. He handed over a few bills and she handed back a few coins. Where was Mom? We were next, and I only had a few coins in my pocket. The gentleman put all his bags back in his cart and started wheeling away. My heart was pounding.

"

Instead of hearing another person's stories as complaints, what if you consider them stories about violated values that they yearn to restore?

"

"Next!"

It was our turn and Mom wasn't back. The cashier stared at me expectantly, and probably everyone else did, too. I couldn't leave the line because the cashier lane was too narrow and the cart was too heavy. I froze.

"Coming! Coming!"

Mom's voice! I turned quickly, and there she was, running toward me through the crowd, waving a bag of nuts. She gestured for me to begin unloading our groceries. Relieved but still flustered, I pushed the cart forward.

"Sorry, I couldn't find them easily," she said, shrugging nonchalantly. "Your favorite cookies. Let's bake them tonight."

There's always more to a story

Do you know someone who complains a lot? They complain about what's wrong with the world, what's wrong with others, or even what's wrong with themselves. They find endless topics to grumble about. When this person is a family member or friend, we often simply tune out their all-too-familiar but not-so-welcome problem. Sometimes doctors or police officers ask, "What's your complaint?" Or, more diplomatically, "What's the matter?"

If you listen closely to people telling you what's the matter, you'll find *what matters to them* standing right in the middle of their stories.

"What's going on?"

"There's just too much work. I seem to be the only one doing anything, and other people don't even seem to care. Why do I always end up doing everyone else's work?"

"That sounds frustrating. Clearly, that's not something you want to continue."

"Not at all."

"So, what do you want instead of that?"

"Well, if people could just do what they are supposed to do, that'd be nice for a change."

"And suppose they did, why is that important to you, that people do what they're supposed to?"

"Well, it's the fairness of it. Right?"

In the whingeing about bad traffic lives a wish for a better morning; in the lament about a heavy workload is a longing for fairness; in the despair of loneliness stands a desire to connect. Instead of hearing another person's stories as complaints, what if you consider them stories about violated values that they yearn to restore? What if another's unrelenting complaints are actually passionate appeals for positive change?

Reflection Guide

Sometimes when we put ourselves in other people's stead, we gain useful insights and experiences. Especially seeing "complaints" as an expression of values, ask yourself the following questions to examine your experiences:

- When have you stepped in to resolve an issue or advocate for another person? What deciding factor made you step in? How did things turn out?

- When have you experienced someone else advocating for one of your needs, even a very small one? What was it like for you to have someone else step in your place?

- Think of a habit that you'd like to change. If you could choose what you'd like instead of that habit, what would that be?

Just

Cue new actions by creating a perception
that a proposed action may be effortless.

I F YOU EVER learned to play tennis or the piano or any other skill requiring dexterity, you know how difficult it is to unlearn something. Golf was that for me. Dad taught me when I was fifteen. His lessons were philosophical. He said golf was the only sport where we didn't need a referee because we kept each other in check. He taught me all the manners of the game, but I didn't get better.

When I was twenty-five and could afford an instructor, I signed up for six lessons with a golf pro. Her lessons were mechanical. She made me practice half-swings without hitting the ball for an entire lesson. She taught me all the methods, and I was bored out of my mind. When I was thirty-five and my nephews were old enough for a golf camp, I met their golf teacher, Lexi.

"Hello, boys, nice to meet you," she said.

"Hello, Ms. Lexi," the boys responded.

"Oh, just call me Lexi. So, let me see your golf swings," she said.

"Uh, it's their first time," I replied on their behalf.

"Okay. But you guys have seen a swing before, right?" she asked, and they nodded.

She gestured for me to take a seat behind the safety line.

"Just try it. Show me," she said to Jeremy, handing him a golf club and waving for him to take a stand on the mat. "Here's the ball, just hit it," she added, placing the ball in front of him.

Jeremy looked at me and I nodded. He pulled the club backward and forcefully axed down on the ball, missing it.

"Okay. Gimme one more. Keep your eye on the ball. Just keep your elbows stiff like a board. Go!"

He wiggled his arms and went at it again, this time topping the ball.

"Yay, you touched it! High five, buddy," Lexi said, raising her palm so Jeremy could coyly give her five. "Now, just one more," she said, placing a second ball in front of him. "Keep everything just the same. Look at the ball." Jeremy placed his club behind the ball, ready to roll up.

"Just remember where the ball is," she said, and then, almost hypnotically, "Now, close your eyes."

What? That wasn't even something I could do. I was rather miffed with her, but Jeremy closed his eyes and pulled up the club with his stiff elbows.

"Now, come down and just scoop it up," Lexi whispered.

Eyes still closed, Jeremy threw down the club with a *s-h-o-o-w-h-i-p* that was followed by a tap— the sound of the sweet spot!

"No way!" I said, jumping up. It took a second for Jeremy to realize what had just happened.

"Yehhheees!" he roared with his fist up.

"Yeah, buddy. Just like that," Lexi chuckled as she turned to give me a sportive wink. It was just magical.

Ordinary magic

People who come for coaching often want to see something improve or want to get better at something. A manager wants to build a positive culture. A parent wants to raise a happy family. A couple wants to set healthy boundaries.

"How does that show up?" I ask them.

The manager says it shows up when people say good morning to each other at the start of their workday. The parent says it shows up when the family is present for dinner together. The couple says it shows up when they spend their together-time not talking about each other's work stress.

"Where does that begin?" I follow up.

Like a small fluff of cloud on the horizon that eventually brings refreshing rainfall, how does their change begin with a tiny bit? The manager remembers an occasion when a team member put a message in their team communication logbook: "Good morning" with a smiley face next to it. That day, people said good morning to each other more than usual. Just like that. The parent remembers an occasion when there were no phones during dinner. That night, the family seemed to talk more and shared more jokes over the meal. Just like that. The couple remembers an occasion when they were sorting through a shoebox full of old photographs. Going through them together, they talked about good times they'd had with family and friends. Just like that.

Focus on the stories
that orient our attention to
our preferences, our purpose,
and existing progress in
the right direction.

When we follow the trail of people's hopes and dreams, we arrive at tiny signposts. These are often ordinary occasions that we have already experienced— ones that orient our attention to our preferences, our purpose, and existing progress in the right direction. But, until we are reminded of their significance, we forget to pay attention to those small signs precisely because they are small.

The next time you're in a conversation in which an employee, a partner, a client, or a friend expresses longing for something, just try these questions:

- Where does that show up?
- Where did that begin?

Notice if your inquiry guides them to a place where they've already realized what they yearn for.

Reflection Guide

Think back to a morning you really enjoyed in recent weeks. Maybe things were *just* the way you liked it, wanted it, or planned it.

- What was it about that morning that you most enjoyed? Where did it begin? The night before? The day before? The week leading up to that morning?

- What are some small-but-not-insignificant habits, activities, or routines you have that seem to work for you?

- If you can do just one or two things to have more of those enjoyable mornings, what might that be?

Here is an activity:

- For one week, try a new habit that is small but noticeable: brushing your teeth with your non-dominant hand, keeping one corner of your desk clean at all times, making your bed differently, and so on.

Know

Assume and honor diverse preferences
of interacting with the world.

I STOLE MONEY FROM DAD.

Not that I knew it was money. The coin had such an intricate texture, and four-year-old me wanted to trace it onto thin paper, so I took it from his night table. Before I remembered to return it, Dad summoned me and my two siblings to my parents' room.

"Did you take a coin from this table?" he asked us one by one, in birth order.

"Nope," my sister said light-heartedly.

"Never!" my brother protested confidently.

Then it was my turn. I wasn't sure. Seeing my hesitation, my brother started taunting me.

"You stole it!" he said.

"No, I didn't!" I screamed back, because I hadn't stolen it. I'd just borrowed it.

"Okay. So, no one took it," Dad said. "Well, we have a simple way to find out," he added with what I recall was a slight smile. "Each of you, go get a raw egg."

"What will a raw egg do, Dad?" my brother asked.

"You'll poke a little hole and drink a little from the egg. Whoever is not telling the truth, their mouth will turn black."

"Wicked!" my siblings chimed in unison as they scurried to the fridge.

"Aren't you gonna get one?" Dad asked as I dilly-dallied.

"No, my tummy hurts," I said, and my tummy really was churning at the thought of the egg-turned-tar in my mouth.

Dad promptly dismissed my heckling siblings and told me he wanted to talk.

"My tummy hurts!" I screamed.

"I'll wait till you're ready," he said with a loving smile.

And he did wait, until my sobs changed to occasional hiccups. Then we talked. I don't remember our exact words, but I do remember his big loving embrace and knowing I was loved no matter what.

Learn another's logic of doing their life

There are different ways of knowing. My mechanic's way of knowing my car might not be the same as my mother's way of knowing my heart. The root word of "know," *gno*, is found in many other words, like "gnome" and "ignore." Other combinations of this root make familiar English words rather curious. Take, for example, "diagnose." The root word *dia-* means through or thorough; when put together with *-gnose*, we get a descriptive action: thoroughly know. When someone's diagnosing something, who does the work of thoroughly knowing? In a medical setting, the doctor's job is to thoroughly know. So, doctors ask questions. Many questions. They need to gather enough information so that they can reach a conclusion—a diagnosis—and, hopefully, prescribe treatment. Doctors may know how to treat the frozen shoulder of a patient in her seventies, but they may not know that this loving grandma wants her shoulders to work so she can cook her grandchildren's favorite meals again.

Unless you ask, you don't know the other person's logic for their life.

When you uphold the
other as the expert of
doing their life, you can get
curious about their way
of "being" and "doing"
(their logic) in the world.

When you uphold the other as the expert of doing their life, you can get curious about their way of "being" and "doing" (their logic) in the world. You can approach your conversations with an authentic learning stance, assuming that they must have a good reason for wanting what they want and doing what they do, as I did with Helena when I asked, "Suppose our conversation somehow turns out to be useful. How might you *know* that things are moving in the right direction for you?"

"Well, I might be more patient with my shoulder recovery. It's just taking so long." She shrugged.

"More patience, okay," I said. "What else?"

"If I could be more motivated to follow those exercises they gave me, that would be nice."

"More motivated about those exercises," I repeated her words, and then inferred, "Okay. So, you want to get better soon."

"Of course I do," Helena confirmed.

"You do! So, what are some things that you want to do first when you get better?"

This last question assumes that Helena might like to do certain things when her shoulder is better. She might have her own "If this happens, then I will..."

logic that I need to learn about. In answering this, Helena tells me several stories about, "If my shoulders get better, then I will..." She wants to cook for her grandchildren. She'll play golf with her children. She'll go about her life with more independence. She'll garden.

Clients, employees, friends, and family often have good ideas about how they want things to be different or even better. Listening more intentionally for what they care about makes it easier to discover their preferences and resources—their life logic.

My conversation with Helena continued. I asked, "And what are you already doing that you know is helpful in that direction?"

"Oh," she said, "I don't like to do those exercises at home because it's stuffy. I go for a walk outside. That moves my arms and I can breathe. I stretch in the morning. It's similar to those exercises anyway."

That people are already doing things that work in their lives should not be surprising. When other people offer their well-informed advice—even if it comes from a medical specialist, a parent, or a supervisor—we follow them in the way that makes sense to us. All the details that didn't fit into the fifteen-minute appointment slot with the doctor were Helena's very own ways of getting better.

"So, Helena, as we wrap up our conversation today, what has been specifically useful for you?"

"Hmm. Good question," she said and took a long pause to think about it. "Now I know why I need to want to do what I knew I had to do." She laughed. "Tongue twister. Did you get that?"

Reflection Guide

Changing the narrative from "ought to do" to "want to do" is not always easy. That shift might even trump goals and action steps. Here are some ways that we can begin to shift:

- You might be hesitant to act, despite knowing it would serve you and others well. Suppose you somehow wake up tomorrow morning ready to do something you've been resistant to. What will the first hour of your morning look like? What will you be doing more of and less of?

- Suppose some inanimate objects around you come alive (the walls, the bed, your notebook, your socks). What will they hear or see you do or say when you go about your day the way you genuinely want?

- Based on some of the observations above, what do you notice that you truly care about?

Look

Articulate internal experiences and impressions;
externalize these as behaviors and interactions.

THE YEAR 2020 was not an easy one. Early in the year I found myself sitting in a blood clinic as COVID-19 was making its way to my hometown of Toronto, Canada. Beside me sat an elderly Asian man with a blue paper mask and a frequent chest cough. People gave the man "the look" before hurriedly moving to new seats as far from him as possible, covering their faces with scarves, gloves, and sleeves. Who could blame them? The old man wore the face of COVID-19. And yet, I felt the urge to speak up.

"Hey, everyone."

They looked up, a bit surprised.

"I know he looks and sounds like he's got coronavirus."

Now they appeared a bit nervous and somewhat annoyed.

"This is my dad. He's battling lung cancer. Please relax."

Following a brief processing pause, some made a "whatever" face and some turned back to their phone screens. I felt many more words stuck somewhere between my throat and my chest, and I shook my head in disbelief at what we'd just experienced. As I turned to Dad to check on him, I noticed a woman who sat a few rows away gazing at us. She sat with a man I took to be her husband. She nodded and smiled and, when she leaned forward a bit, her seat began to roll. She was in a wheelchair! She steered herself over to me.

"You know… every time I go to a clinic with my husband, they think I'm the patient. In fact, I'm here for my husband, who's battling cancer also. Well, your dad has the look of coronavirus. I got the one for disability," she chuckled.

What a relief.

"I know, maybe we should get a T-shirt that says, 'It's not me, it's you,'" I joked, and we laughed. The mood around us improved but my heart wept. For the first time in my life, in the city I call home, I experienced the silent violence of discrimination because of how we looked.

66

When you change
another person's words
by adding your own words,
you actively generate a new
possibility in shaping their
world—sometimes usefully,
sometimes dreadfully.

99

Our words generate our worlds

It might be a centuries-old story, but to some of us it isn't. How many times have we unknowingly or silently participated in creating, confirming, and perpetuating biases? When you hear words like "violent person" or "disabled" or "someone with authority," what images come to your mind immediately? Coaching conversations are not necessarily free of biased exchanges in which we quickly form inaccurate impressions of the other. From the moment we first start a conversation, our biases inform our perceptions: of what kind of person they might be, what they should want for life, what they might need from us, or what they mean by what they say.

Take, for example, a conversation between me and Zein, a coaching student who came in for mentorship. Zein brought along a video recording of a session with a client who was working as a CEO. I asked Zein about the session before we started watching.

"How was your session, Zein?" I said.

My student looked rather frazzled. "Whew, that really was one tough client. That CEO challenged everything I said, and I can see how difficult it might be to work for someone like that."

"Okay, we'll watch the tape together. So, what do you think went well in the session?"

"Well, the fact that neither of us walked away in the middle of it was a good sign. Believe me, I almost did. It was frustrating," Zein said, plopping into a chair next to me.

I laughed, "Okay. Let's see the tape." And Zein started to play the recording.

Now, dear reader, let me ask you this: At this point, as you imagine the scene between Zein and me, and the one on the video between Zein and the CEO, who do you see? What does Zein look like? What does the CEO look like? What do they sound like? What genders, ethnicities, and ages does your imagination render? When Zein began to play the recording, I momentarily thought he had brought the wrong one. (Yes, Zein is a he.) He sat with a petite black woman, probably in her seventies. She was so soft-spoken we had to increase the volume when watching the video.

CEO: The board hired me to make some very necessary changes, but when I propose specifics, they push back. I don't think they're ready for it.

Zein: So, how do you need to communicate better so that it's not too aggressive?

CEO: Aggressive? I'm not aggressive.

Zein: No, I mean, the changes. You need their buy-in.

CEO: No, I'm doing exactly what they asked for. It's quite the opposite of aggressive.

Zein: Do you think you need to be more assertive about how you communicate?

CEO: Not at all. You might be inferring that because I'm soft-spoken, right?

Zein stopped the video.

"See how resistant she is?" he asked, seeking my agreement.

What do you see in this short excerpt of the conversation between Zein and the CEO?

The illusion of resistance consistently happens when you interpret and infer based on what another person says. How irritating can it be when someone rephrases your words and interprets your meaning without your permission or confirmation—or when they get it all wrong? Honoring another person's words as a useful reference to their worldview is one of the most difficult things to learn in coaching conversations.

Take what happened between Zein and the CEO. What words did Zein add to this conversation? How did it work? He assumed that she *needs to communicate better,* inferring that she currently is *too aggressive*; and she disagrees with his suggestion about her character. Zein gives it another try, questioning whether she needs to *be more assertive* when she communicates. She disagrees with that suggestion, too. Zein added those words. His client disagreed with them. And he then called her resistant!

When you change another person's words by adding your own words, you actively generate a new possibility in shaping their world—sometimes usefully, sometimes dreadfully. The fact that you know the common dictionary definition of a word doesn't mean you know what another person means when using the word—we each have our own lexicon. How I define "content" or "aggressive" in my personal dictionary might be quite different from your definitions, for example. So, when you hear what others say, consider that as an invitation to inquire about what they mean in their world, not as permission to impose meaning from your world. In conversation, ask, "When you say [insert the words they used], what does that look like? What does that mean to you?"

Reflection Guide

Here's a reflective activity for you to pay attention to the words that fill you internally and surround you externally.

- Write down a list of fifty words (adjectives, nouns, verbs) to describe yourself. You can interview your friends/family/colleagues who know you fairly well to build your list. Choose up to five words you hope to see increased in your life. Using these five words, write a short bio, just a few sentences long.

Might

Open up possibilities by
staying tentative and curious.

"**M**OMMY, GUESS WHAT happened in my dream last night."

Often this was my opening line for the day as I awoke as a four-year-old. "Tell me what happened," she would say as my tiny body scooted over to make room for her and she reclined on my child-sized bed.

"So, here's what happened..."

I would begin to tell her everything I remembered from my dream, and as I told, some parts already became hazy. "And then?" she would nudge me as she listened with such curious "mhms" and "ahs." By the time my dream-telling had taken several "and then" turns, my story would be clearer than my dream. "Well, that really is a good dream. You know why?" she'd add after every dream I told her about, and she gave each dream a reason for being a good one. Flying meant I was getting taller, picking flowers meant good news on its way, and teeth falling out meant resolved problems (whatever the problems may be for a four-year-old). Then one day I had a dream of tripping down the stairs, and as she responded in her usual way, I challenged her.

"But Mommy, how can this be a good dream? Didn't you say last time that climbing the stairs was a good dream? This is the opposite of that."

"Well…" she said with her eyebrows slightly raised, then a smile, "look closely. It's a different staircase, my love." And there it was, a different staircase, as if it was simply forgotten in my dream etching its way back to my memory. Mom made every dream matter, and she taught me that there was always another way to look at it.

The might of *might*

My coaching clients bring lots of, "So, here's what happened," stories to our sessions. Some seem readier with their stories than others; some stories sound better rehearsed than others. As they narrate, often I sit with those "mhms" and "ahs" at every turn they make. I am curious not about what happened but more about how they want their stories to end. So, I ask, "Suppose, just suppose... somehow this story ends in a way that makes your heart sing. What might you notice that's even better or different than how it has been?" And I see my clients sit with their own echoes of a new story. Their stories now detour from their familiar routes. As I nudge them along with the occasional, "And then what might happen?" I get a tour of their hopes and dreams in their own curated way that gives me a glimpse of what they truly care about. Now they tell a story of *what matters* instead of *what's the matter* in their life, and the session comes to an end so that their life may begin.

When people are invited to prospect (think about the future), they often start with an immediate topic. They'd show up at work the next day with peace. They'd walk into that interview with confidence. They'd step into their class with motivation.

People often mistake that immediate topic as the *destination* of the person speaking, and they start problem-solving *toward* it. In coaching, we take that topic as another *departure point* on people's way to their desired direction and start building *from* it.

"

In coaching, we take people's initial topic as their *departure point*, not a destination. We assume they are already moving in their desired direction and start building *from* it.

"

In conversation, try asking questions like, "Suppose you show up at work with that peace?" instead of, "How will you get that peace?" Ask, "Suppose you walk into that interview with confidence?" instead of, "How will you gain that confidence?" Ask, "Suppose you step into your class with motivation?" instead of, "How will you get that motivation?" Once your conversation partner supposes their preferred future, you can simply invite them to imagine "What might happen next?" in their life when—not if—the preferred future is happening.

Reflection Guide

Think about a tough conversation that you need to have with someone; a talk that might not be easy but is necessary.

- Suppose that conversation goes well, leaving both of you feeling uplifted, grateful, and relieved. What might be some additional positive effects of that conversation?

Notice

Attend to the signs of purpose, progress,
possibilities, priorities, and preferences
embedded in others' stories.

a b c
d e f g h
i j k l m
n o p q r
s t u v w
x y z

WE GAVE HER a nickname: Detective Mom. Even though she was at work all day, she knew everything the moment she stepped into the house: what we had eaten, if we had fought, if we had watched TV instead of doing our homework. She offered me snacks before I knew I was getting hungry. She gave me her time just when I was becoming angry or sad. She even knew when I tried smoking for the first time, despite my having so thoroughly washed the smell off my hands and out of my hair. How did she know?

I eventually moved on from juvenile subterfuges. By the time I started university and lived away from home for the first time, I was ready for my grown-up life full of grown-up stuff. Then, in third year, it happened: a relationship that was more than friendship but couldn't be love. My first heartbreak.

Bewildered, I lost all appetite for food and sleep. I avoided phone calls, and days passed without my talking to anyone.

Then, one evening, the black-corded phone on the wall of my dark and messy bachelor apartment rang. I didn't get up from my chair, hoping it would stop ringing. Five rings and it stopped. I sighed. It started ringing again, and I groaned as I rose in annoyance and took labored steps toward the phone. It rang a fifth and then a sixth time as I squinted my eyes to see the call display screen: "Home," it read. On the seventh ring, I put my hand on the receiver, debating. *It's probably Mom*, I thought. I cleared my throat and picked up.

"Hello," I said, trying to sound chirpy and like I was in the middle of something important.

"Hello, our baby."

That was one of many terms of endearment my parents used with me. Mom sounded quiet and kind. I felt the heat around my eyes. I wanted to flop onto the floor and just let it all out. But I held everything together. I couldn't quite say anything.

"We're just leaving now. See you in an hour, our princess."

I was only an hour's drive away, and on Sundays they delivered home-cooked meals and groceries.

"Is today Sunday?" I asked.

There was a brief pause. Maybe I shouldn't have asked. I looked up to the wall calendar that hadn't been turned to this month.

"Today's Friday, love. And, in fact, we'd really love it if you'd come home this weekend."

I wanted to, but I didn't want to. I worried that I might upset them. I opened my mouth to say, "No, don't come."

"Arong might come, too," Mom added.

My dog? My face remembered to smile at her name. My parents rarely brought the little terrier along for the long drive.

"Okay. That's fine." I wasn't sure what was fine, but I okayed it. "Buzz me when you get here," I mumbled. "I'll come down." I didn't want them to come up and see the mess.

After I hung up the phone, I turned on the lights and started gathering laundry to bring home. I didn't want to come back to a foul-smelling apartment, so I put out the garbage. I collected all the glasses and mugs spread around the room and did the dishes, too. I put on my wristwatch to track the time so they wouldn't have to wait downstairs. I was quite tired by the time I climbed into the car with two loads of laundry and my backpack. After a quick hello to my parents and my dog, who was ecstatic to see me, I fell asleep in the back seat with Arong curled up in my lap. I vaguely remember getting home and crawling into the fresh-laundry scent of my bedsheets. I slept, almost until midday, when I woke to find Arong beside me and the aroma of fresh coffee and baking wafting from the kitchen to my bedroom. I was so hungry.

"Hi, Mom," I said, as I stepped into the kitchen.

"Hi there, sleepyhead. Did you sleep well?" she asked, smiling and glancing at me quickly as she poured a freshly brewed jug of coffee into a large travel Thermos.

"Yeah, I did." And I had. It'd been a while since I'd slept so well.

"Well, I want to take you out on a date today, just you and me." She held up the Thermos and her car keys.

Following a quick bite, we hopped into the car. Mom drove for nearly two hours, neither of us saying very much. When we reached the shores of Lake

Simcoe, she parked at a quiet strip of beach where I could just sit and think alone. She'd packed a beach blanket, hot café mocha, and light snacks. She sat nearby with a book, but far enough away to give me my own space. About the time I began to feel the autumn sunset on my cheeks, Mom seemed to be finishing her last few pages. I got up and stretched in the orange sun. Mom looked up and smiled. *What a perfect bystander who always stands by me*, I thought.

"Shall we?" I asked, smiling back.

Believing is seeing

I remember meeting Judy, who was passionate about her work as an executive director at a general hospital. She was in her second month in the role when she called to speak with me, and she sounded frustrated.

"The hospital is so disorganized and outdated. It's unbelievable. Like, are we living in the seventies or what?" she said.

"Wow, it sounds like you've got some work to do there."

"Believe me, it's crazy. Everything needs to change. Everything needs to be done over again."

66

You learn to stand
by, attending to the
progress of others,
rather than assessing
them constantly.

99

I was struck by the tone of her frustration as she spoke. "That's a big job," I said. "Where do you begin?"

"That's where I'm stuck," Judy sighed. "They're so resistant. How can they not see it? I feel like I'm the only one who can see through it all, and it's so frustrating."

Judy seemed to have a vision of what needed to be done, and she was struggling with people not seeing it nor agreeing with her.

Where do you go from here with a frustrated person who feels stuck and wants everyone else to change? At the end of our call, I proposed a simple task she could experiment with. "Suppose you have the power to change anything that you want at your work."

"Gosh," Judy said, "wouldn't that be nice."

I continued, "Even with that power to change everything, could you please make a note of what you might keep as is?"

"Huh? What I might not change?"

"Yes, it can be something as small as the location of a trash can. Something that you wouldn't change because it's working well as is. Could you please make a note of those things at your work?"

She sounded skeptical. "Uh, it'll be hard."

"Yes, it might be." I smiled on the other end of the line. "Just give it a try. And whenever you notice it, tell someone about it."

Judy agreed to do the experimental homework until we met again in three weeks. The morning of our follow-up call, I was wondering how her experiment had gone when the telephone rang.

"Haesun, I don't know what happened." No hint of frustration in Judy's voice! She sounded elated, perhaps even surprised. "Since we talked, something changed."

"What do you mean?"

"Well, I realized that we have very competent people on our team. And things aren't that bad, actually. I just didn't see all the details before."

"Wow, that sounds exciting. So, what do you want to change?"

"Probably a few things, but I'll leave it up to the team to make recommendations. They know what they're doing."

Our follow-up call was short. But our conversation resonated with me long after the call, and hopefully for Judy and her team, too.

When you witness small-but-not-insignificant details that are working well, you become primed to notice differently. You learn to stand by, attending to the progress of others, rather than assessing them constantly. Try this as you go about your day and, after a week, take stock of what changed for the better. What do you notice now that you didn't notice before?

Reflection Guide

Whether excited or worried, you have a way of knowing and showing how you are doing. Think back on a time when you were having one of those moments (preferably, a moment of joy).

- What was happening?

- What did you notice about yourself immediately that other people may not notice readily?

- Who was the first to notice something "different" about you? What did they notice?

- How do people get to know how you are doing? What would be your preferred way of knowing and showing that?

Opposite

Accentuate what's wanted (positive changes) by
juxtaposing what's not wanted (negative changes).

"MOMMY, WHO'S YOUR favorite?" I used to ask every now and then.

"You are, my baby."

I'd then go about my day with my nose up a bit and my chest puffed out a bit. My two siblings were too old to be playing my child's game, but I knew I was her favorite. Because she told me so. Then one day I was playing in the living room while my brother was helping Mom in the kitchen.

"Mom," my brother said.

"Yes, my love?" she responded while her whisk played the edges of a metal bowl.

"So, who's your favorite?"

What?

I stopped my play and turned my head just enough to tune in to their conversation. I already knew I was her favorite, but my ears leaned in to hear the answer.

"You are, my love," she said.

What?

My heart sank. What was this feeling? It felt like I'd just lost something. I ran to the kitchen in distress.

"M-a-a-a-a-h-m..."

"Oh, hey there, my baby," she said, turning toward me as I held up my arms to wrap around her hips. She rubbed my head with her elbow, trying to not get flour on my baby-blue summer dress. I buried half my face in her checkered red apron that smelled faintly of vanilla, squeezing her as tightly as I could and cutting one eye at my brother to see if he was watching. He wore a slight smirk as he peeled potatoes, like nothing had happened.

"What's going on, my baby?" Mom asked, hugging my head between her waist and elbow.

"Nothing. I'm just tired," I whimpered as I rubbed my face on her side.

"Is everything okay?" she asked in a soothing tone.

"Hmph!" I whined a bit louder than intended.

"Hmm..." She pulled away from me and bent down so her face was close to my face. "What's going on?"

"Can I speak to you in private, please?" I mumbled, turning away from my brother.

"Now? Is this very important? I'm in the middle of making your favorite cookie dough."

"Yes, it is!" I said, stomping my foot.

"Okay then. Calvin, would you please excuse us?"

"Sure, Mom," he said, sounding chipper. He got up from his chair and left the kitchen.

"Yes?" Mom asked, resting one elbow on the table and looking at me with raised eyebrows. I looked up at her when I heard a door closing.

"Mommy, I'm your favorite, right?"

"Yes, you are, my baby," she said, her eyes rounding to crescents.

"But you just told Calvin he was your favorite. Who's your favorite? Me or him?" My heart was racing. I needed an answer. She needed to choose.

"Don't be frowny," she said and kissed my forehead. "My baby, both of you. All of you. Whoever is in front of me is my favorite."

Putting the difference to work

A fascinating aspect of my work is witnessing the unfolding and winding of many stories as my clients navigate through their situations. Some deliberate

turns in their story, like important decisions or resolutions, make them sit up a little taller, while some
unexpected turns, like silly mistakes or loss, make
them smile or sigh. Either way, those turns are simply a metaphor for their progress.

In coaching, to help clients visualize their progress, I often use a scale that runs from ten to one,
with ten being the positive end and one being the
opposite. I invite people to describe their ten in great
detail, while the one is left vague, just the "opposite"
of their ten.

One young student described her ten as her
friendships deepening with two other students at
her new school. In her life at ten, they'd eat lunch
together on the bench outside. They'd meet by the
main staircase and walk home together after school.
A teacher described his ten as feeling confident on
his first day of teaching high school. He'd be smiling
and making eye contact with the students; he would
wave and say, "Hello everyone," as he walked in. He'd
move the lectern out of the way so that he could stand
before the class without any barrier between them.
When you use a simple conversational tool like a
scale, asking people to describe their life at ten in

vivid detail, you are inviting them to perform their preferred future in their imagination. And that imagination is often closely linked with existing experiences they may have forgotten about. The following is one such example from a coaching conversation:

Coach: So, on a scale of ten to one, if ten is the scenario you were describing [the development of friendships or the confident first day of teaching, for example], and one is the opposite of that, where would you say you are today?

Client: I'm at about a four.

Coach: Would you say that four is high for you or low for you?

Client: Oh, it's pretty low.

Coach: Oh, okay. So, you've been higher on the scale before.

Client: I think so.

Coach: Okay. So, as you think a bit more about it, what was the highest number on that scale you think you've ever experienced, even very briefly?

Whichever number a
person is at on the scale
is a metaphor of progress,
not regress. Explore what's
already there, not what needs
to be there to be higher.

Client: I'd say about . . . at least an eight or even a nine, once or twice.

Coach: Wow, okay. And when was that?

Client: Well, about two weeks ago.

And your conversation partner unpacks the stories of those times when they were already moving toward ten. Like the young student remembering outdoor lunch on one sunny day last week. Or the teacher remembering the open house two weeks ago welcoming the new students to the high school. The opposite of ten on a scale is simply a point of reference for their own measure of progress. Any number on the scale higher than that opposite is simply an invitation to inquire about their progress. Even when they say they are at the lowest end of the scale, you can inquire into how they manage to cope with it, what helps them keep from getting lower, how they look toward what they want despite the current situation. Whichever number is in front of them is a metaphor of progress, not regress.

Reflection Guide

You may have found yourself up against some challenges in your life (relational, vocational, physical, financial, or even spiritual) that turned out to be meaningful after you were through. Maybe you walked away from something. Maybe you leaped into something. Now reflect on one such occasion.

- How did you decide to participate in or contribute to the experience?

- What signals began to tell you that it was turning out "right" or "better"?

- In what ways are you still benefiting from that experience?

Possible

Invite others to perform their preferred future
by using what's both possible and useful.

HOW DO YOU do your grocery shopping? Some do it on scheduled days at the same stores, a written list in hand. Some do it at random times at convenient locations, often forgetting their lists at home or in their car. That's me—spontaneous and opportunistic. I don't have a set day or particular stores that I frequent. Take, for instance, my great corn-on-the-cob misadventure.

On my way home from an out-of-town training session, I saw a hand-painted sign by the roadside that said "Fresh Corn on the Cob." I wanted some, so I pulled into the small parking lot of the barn-like shop with a family restaurant attached to it. A bustling market always brings back sweet memories of tailing Mom around the market when I was a kid. Even before I entered the shop, I smelled smoked ham and rotisserie chicken, maybe from the restaurant next door. I entered to discover the market was surprisingly big inside. Three cashier stations on my left were busy with customers, but no one seemed to be in a rush. On my right were rows of carts and stacks of baskets. How heavy could corn be?

I grabbed a basket. There appeared to be about eight aisles in the store, and I started browsing aisle by aisle. It wasn't as though I had to rush anywhere. The first aisle was stationery and hardware. *That seems odd for a farmer's market*, I thought. Duct tape was on sale. I needed that. I could strengthen a few loose shelves in the garage. Twenty-five percent off, too. Not bad. With that, the first item went in my basket. The next aisle was baking. I don't bake, but baking soda was on sale and perfect for deodorizing the fridge.

I rounded the corner and found myself in produce. *This is more like it.* "Locally Sourced," a sign proudly boasted. I saw potatoes, cabbages, carrots, and even some ginger. I love potato soup and ginger carrot juice. I love steamed cabbage rolls. Soon my small basket was almost overflowing with ingredients, as was my head with exciting possibilities. On my way to the cashier, a small bunch of lemons looked up at me, full and fresh. *Those will make a wonderful hot tea.* I picked up the lemons and carried them in my free hand.

As I approached the front of the store, I heard shoppers laughing at a cashier's jokes. It felt like one of those friendly small shops you see on TV. I stepped forward when the middle-most cashier waved goodbye to an elderly couple.

"Hi there," I said, putting down the lemons so I could use both hands to swivel the heavy basket onto the counter.

"Hello," she said in a curious and pleasant tone as she began to ring up the groceries. "Fish and chips tonight?"

"Huh?"

"It looks like you're making fish and chips, and maybe coleslaw?"

"Erm..." I looked at the groceries, slightly hesitant. "You can make that with this?"

"Well, you're missing fish, but we don't carry that here," she said, laughing.

"Wow, I didn't think of that. I guess I could."

As I returned to my car with a heavy bagful of unplanned groceries, I realized I'd forgotten to pick up the corn! Instead of going back in, I opened the trunk and loaded up the groceries. Now I had to be somewhere. I had to get to a fish market while one was still open so I could make fish and chips for dinner.

Naming dreams, taming dreads

Imagining what's possible sometimes motivates us. At other times it mortifies us. Our dreams and dreads are often an expression of what we truly care about. A dream of winning a lottery was an expression of Jacob's wish for dignity and respect. A dread of losing her job was Ginny's deepest wish to take care of her children. Andy, a second-year university student, dreaded an exam because of what failure might mean to their dream.

"I'm so worried that I might fail the final next week," Andy said in our session.

"What's your exam on next week?" I asked.

"Microbiology."

"Wow, microbiology." I was impressed. "That doesn't sound easy," I said.

"No, not at all," Andy laughed. "But I like it."

"You do?"

Dreams and
dreads are similar
in their magnitude,
just different in their
frequency.

"Yes, I really do. But it's not easy, and I don't feel ready." They fiddled with a loose thread on their jeans.

"So, doing well on the exam is very important for you?"

"Yes, because the grades I get in this exam will determine my future, pretty much."

"What do you mean?"

"Well, based on the grades, I get to go into specialization in biochemistry or else I have to take a general stream next year."

"So," I said, "you want to get into that specialization."

I have learned that, often in considering what's possible, dreads lurk behind dreams. In this brief conversation, Andy treaded between dread and dream. They wanted to specialize in biochemistry the following year. That was their bright dream in the present. Then the worries trailed along—*What if the exam is too difficult? What if I am not ready enough? What if I fail the exam?*—like the shadow of that dream.

Dreams and dreads are similar in their magnitude, just different in their frequency. Perhaps the most useful stance that you can take in your presence with others is tuning in and resonating at the frequency that amplifies their dreams.

In conversations, you can follow the light rather than the shadows. You can acknowledge the shadows as reflections of people standing in and facing their light. As you unpack their loads, they quickly come to realize that their mortifying worries represent how much they care, and their worries can add fuel to motivate them.

Reflection Guide

You may have certain worries that begin with "What if…" You may also have certain wishes that begin with "If only…" Behind those possibilities lie your deepest cares.

- What concerns you at this moment? Please write down your concerns, or say them aloud.

- For every concern, ask the following questions:

   1 Why is this concern important? (Feel free to repeat this question several times.)

   2 What do you seem to care most about? Be precise and detailed.

   3 What difference would it make for you if this was no longer a concern?

Try this experiment in acting as if:

- Suppose your words have the power to cast a certain spell to make things come true. What would you say to yourself and others throughout the day?

Question

Seek what's useful and necessary for the other
to navigate toward their preferred destination.

WHEN YOU TRAVEL, what do you carry in your suitcase? Do you travel light or heavy? When you pack for a trip, what secret, handy things do you put in your suitcase?

I pack a few spoonfuls of citric acid in a zip-up plastic bag, in case I have to clean a kettle at a hotel. I toss in dryer sheets to keep my suitcase and everything in it smelling fresh. I also pack biodegradable doggie poop bags, I kid you not. I've used them to wrap flip-flops wet from a stroll along the shore in Cancún, to collect crumbs and crunches on a week-long road trip to the Rockies, and for dirty laundry.

My travel companions often tease me about my just-in-case suitcase, but wait long enough and someone needs a pill for their headache or a bandage for their cut or, yes, even a safety pin! I'm probably like this because I grew up with a grandma who always carried a large shoulder bag full of small pouches containing remedies for every complaint.

"Nana, my tummy hurts."

She reaches into her bag for tiny mint candies.

"Nana, I'm hot."

She pulls from her bag a little fan that carries a faint fragrance in the breeze it blows.

"Nana, I'm hungry."

She suddenly produces rice cakes sticking to the wrapper; on long trips there are even boiled eggs that stink up the car.

She got smaller as we got taller, but her bag seemed to grow ever bigger. She came to stay for a few days each month, her magic bag full of my favorite snacks. Occasionally, she carried delightful surprises, like my very first Walkman cassette player! How did she know yellow was the very color I wanted?

When I turned sixteen, my parents decided to immigrate to Canada. When we were getting ready to move to Toronto, my parents asked Grandma if she'd like to stay in Korea or move with us to this new country she'd never heard of. She didn't speak English. She didn't know how to drive. She didn't know anyone in Canada. But she said yes, and we moved to

Canada. For the next ten years, my grandma mostly stayed home. When I moved away to university, she stayed home, where she busied herself with cooking my favorite meals. After I got a job and moved out, I visited her a few days a month with rice cakes and mint candies, her favorite snacks (or so I thought). I took her to the nearby mall to shop, but she rarely bought anything, saying she didn't need anything. She just wanted to walk with me.

Then one day I got a call. She'd had a stroke overnight. I dropped everything and rushed to the hospital. It was all too soon and all too late. On my way to the hospital, I tried to remember the last time I'd told her how much I loved her and wanted to tell her how sorry I was that I hadn't spent more time with her.

The doctors asked me far too many questions I didn't know how to answer, while she remained unconscious. They told me to go to the house and return with a few things that were important to her. All I could think of was her Bible.

I rushed home and ran up to her room, where I saw an unusual disorder, a sign of the paramedics having rushed her out. She had converted the walk-in closet into a prayer room. I opened the door to look for her Bible. A handful of clothes and bags occupied one small corner of the closet. The Bible sat open on a small table, a pencil resting in the crease. She probably had sat right there the night before. I picked it up, closed it, and put it in my backpack. Then, as I turned to step out of the closet, I saw it: a time-worn but familiar shoulder bag hanging on a hook.

"My gosh," I said aloud as I reached for the magic bag, as if to wake it up.

It rustled under my fingers. It wasn't empty. I carefully lifted it from its hook, folded the flap over the snap button, and opened the mouth to look inside. I found her expired passport, black and white photos of Grandpa, some faded photos of Mom and Dad, some not-so-faded photos of my sister, brother, and me, and photos of my grandmother's friends, some of whom I'd never before seen. I also found every single card that I'd ever given her on her birthday, on Mother's Day, and at Christmas. They were all there among other special cards she had kept. I should have been rushing back to the hospital, but, instead, I stood there feeling her presence, heartbroken by the weight of her love.

"

Within each question
you ask is an embedded
quest of your own curiosity
and assumed request
that your conversation
partner answer it.

"

Reload your question
with useful assumptions

There's a quest in every question. Even when we don't know it, our questions are loaded with assumptions that take up inner and in-between spaces. I often challenge my classes to come up with a question that's neutral enough to be without assumptions. Students usually come back with things like *How are you?* or *What's your name?* or *What day is it today?* Yes, these may seem to be a friendly acknowledgment of another, or at least we mean these questions to be that way. But after my grandma's passing, when I was asked, that innocent "How are you?" was sharp enough to pierce my grieving heart.

Here are a few of the most popular opening questions many counselors and therapists ask their clients:

- What brings you in today?

- How can I help you?

- How are you feeling?

What do these questions assume?

"What brings you in today?" assumes something caused them to visit. It also includes the possibility that it was not by their choice. "How can I help you?" assumes they need help, that the asker can help, and that the person asked knows what help they need. "How are you feeling?" may assume that talking about feelings would be useful.

These are the quests—or explicit re-quests—for information that you might believe will be useful for a conversation. And conversation often ensues because people answer these questions without questioning them.

Coach: How can I help you?

Client: Well, I was hoping you would help me with deciding about...

By answering, the client implicitly agrees to the embedded assumptions that they need help, that the coach can help, and that the client knows what they need help with. The coach's assumptions now became a mutually agreed understanding of identity, capacity, desires, and roles. That's how our words shape our world and how our questions work to shape it. Yes, the saying "You get what you ask for" is, in fact, what happens with people using questions in conversations.

This incredibly complex dance between questions and answers comes about in ordinary corners of our lives. Within each question you ask is an embedded quest of your own curiosity and assumed request that your conversation partner answer it. No wonder some questions feel more like an intrusion than an invitation! If you'd like, observe what you are asking and what you are asking for in your conversations with others. How does the way you frame the question influence the course of the conversation?

Reflection Guide

Ask your family or close friends one or more of these casual questions, starting with, "I have a question for you":

- What was a particularly nice memory from today [at school, at work, at home]?

- What are some things you learned in the last [day, week, or month] that you are now able to do but that you didn't know how to do before?

- What are you most looking forward to?

- What's becoming clearer about [your values, your situation, your decisions] that's important to you?

- What keeps you going, even when things get tough?

Recent

Re-author people's narratives by
reminding them of their resourcefulness.

"**D**ADDY, TELL ME a story." This was how my favorite weekend bedtime ritual began.

Mom read me books, but I already knew all the endings. Listening to familiar stories helped me fall asleep. But Dad's stories kept me so awake that I was allowed them only on weekends. He didn't read them from books. He told them.

His stories often began the same way: brave young scholars travel far, far away to find a secret that could save their people. But the endings were always different, and I stayed wide-eyed until the young heroes brought home the secret.

In one story, the hero brought back a lamp with an undying fire. In another, the hero returned with a magical set of flint stones with healing power. The heroes always arrived at the eleventh hour of some calamity—with sparks and the smell of fire, with the sighs of relief and the cheers of the villagers as they showed up just in the nick of time.

In one such story, the hero returned to find a villain and his henchmen holding all the villagers hostage near the town's gate. The villagers were shivering from the cold of the night and from fear.

"Here I am. Leave them alone," our hero announced.

The henchmen surrounded the hero with swords drawn, and the villain slowly approached. *Thump, thump.*

The henchmen cleared a path for the villain to stand before the hero, the villain's scarred face menacing in the swaying torchlight. He looked down at the hero with a grimace before hissing his threat.

I shuddered myself, feeling the chill of his breath. Our hero reached into a threadbare cloak and withdrew a scroll tied with a golden string. She held it up to the villain's face, then took one end of the string and pulled it. The scroll unwound and the villagers gasped.

It was blank.

The villain growled in fury and raised his sword to strike down the hero.

"Wait!" the hero commanded. "Give me a torch."

With the villain's sword still raised, someone handed our hero a torch.

She carefully illuminated the scroll from behind, and magical gold letters appeared. The villain lowered his sword and bent to make out the letters. He read aloud, "Whoever reads this shall be consumed by his own desires tenfold." Before he could utter anything more, the villain fell to his knees, and the scroll collected his last breath.

I squeezed my blanket tightly as the mob scattered in tremendous fear. Justice served, the righteous prevailed.

"What happened to the scroll after, Dad?"

"We don't know. It was a palimpsest," he said, leaning over to kiss my forehead.

"A what?"

"A palimpsest. A thousand-year-old scroll people reused, over and over again."

"But how?"

"You erased what was on it and wrote over it. But you could still see traces of what was there before."

Even in bits and
pieces, people remember
experiences, interactions,
and situations they'd like
to have more of.

Co-construct a preferred past

One of the root meanings of the word "recent" is said to include the ancient Greek word *kainos*, meaning new or fresh. Some others suspect that it might be directly from the Latin word *recens*, which is shared in the English word "rinse." In its different combinations, the word "recent" may be translated as "rinsing it new" or "refreshing" so that you can use over, write over, do over. This is not to assume it is only the regret or grudge that people want to do over; the concept of recent simply offers a chance to rewind to a preferred past to recall those moments that mattered and that a person somehow did not notice before.

Brian came to see my coaching team with a rather thick case file. He had been seen by several therapists and coaches in the previous twelve months. Post-traumatic stress disorder was suspected. The file told me of his trauma story—an accident that had happened during his military deployment. His unit had gone out on a routine patrol one eerily quiet morning just two weeks before his scheduled return home. His dog had suddenly tugged at his leash, and all he remembered after was that he had lost his best buddy and his beloved dog to a roadside landmine that had claimed his own right leg.

Now back in his civilian life, far too many triggers hid in ordinary days. The previous month, he had attempted grocery shopping, but someone had returned a shopping cart, and the clash as one cart hit the next set him off. He'd jumped the perpetrator. The triggers were affecting his family, and he wanted help. As he sat in front us, he opened with a familiar retelling of the events of that eerie morning. I interrupted.

"Brian, it sounds like you've gone through tremendous experiences people like us can't even imagine," I said with genuine concern and appreciation.

"Yeah, you can say that," he said.

"And after going through all that, you are here hoping to make it better for yourself and your family."

"Yeah, sure I am."

"Brian, how do you do this? Where did you learn to be so incredibly resilient?"

Brian furrowed his brow, looked away, and then exhaled deeply through pursed lips. He nodded slightly.

"Well, as I was saying," he said, looking up at me, "that day when I lost Tyler and Max..." (This was a familiar opening, so far.) "I thought that was it for me too, and all I could see were the faces of my family."

All I could say was, "Mhm."

"And I remember that moment. That's when I decided to live. Survive this. I gotta get back to my family. I fought hard. I had no other choice... That's what taught me to be resilient," he said.

Brian continued to tell his story of the accident, but it was now a very different story than what's in his case file: one not of trauma but of resilience. I've seen many clients re-author their narratives like Brian did when invited to remember a recent time when things were moving in their preferred direction.

Ivory, a thirty-seven-year-old lawyer, wanted to reconcile with her brother. She wanted to be able to joke around like they used to. When invited to remember a recent time when she had seen some parts of this already happening, Ivory recalled a family barbeque just two weeks prior, when they'd had fun together, playing Jenga on a picnic table with their nieces. Ayo, a twenty-eight-year-old first-time teacher, wanted more confidence in conversations with a demanding parent, to encourage the parent to be patient with the child's learning progress. Ayo recalled a time recently when the parent had high-fived the child for getting a B+ on a spelling test.

Even in bits and pieces, people remember experiences, interactions, and situations they'd like to have more of. As you invite them to re-author a new story with those bits and pieces, you witness how they turn them into a preferred new story like turning a kaleidoscope. Their new story becomes a new way of making sense of their life.

Reflection Guide

Thinking back on your past week, consider these questions:

- What moments reminded you of what you care about in life?

- What moments gave you a chance to feel refreshed?

- How did you manage to be in those moments?

- What moments do you want to see increase starting next week?

- What seems to be moving in the right direction for you?

Suppose

Suggest that they consider alternate
possibilities in a preferred direction.

HIS PERSISTENT COUGH had worsened in the past few months. His doctor ordered first an X-ray, then CT and PET scans. I didn't know that to be a typical sequence when doctors suspect cancer.

Today's appointment was a follow-up to get the results, and I went with Mom and Dad to translate for them. The oncologist greeted us so cheerfully I thought to myself, *Thank goodness it isn't anything serious*. The doctor began flipping through the pages of her report, and I pulled out my notebook, just in case.

"Unfortunately..."

What a grim word to begin a sentence with, I thought.

"... your father has stage four lung cancer."

All of a sudden, the room felt stuffy and the doctor's voice sounded muffled. I had to interlace my fingers to hide my shiver as I searched for words. Before I could say anything, I felt a gentle tap on my shoulder.

"What's the doctor saying, my dear?" Dad asked.

Right. I'm here to translate, I remembered. *I've just heard the news myself and now I have to tell Dad.*

—

BACK FROM THE exhausting appointment, we were sitting together silently in the living room. The dusk made everything feel weighted as I sat beside Dad, not knowing what to say. The room got heavier and heavier as we three watched the dark settle in.

"Let me get the lights," I finally said, rising from the sofa.

"Do you think it would've made any difference if I'd got it checked earlier?" Dad said without looking up, as if he were asking himself.

That's . . . regret, I told myself.

I felt so thirsty as I walked over to the light switch and flipped it on. The pot lights outlined Dad's slouched frame half-buried in the couch.

"How long do you think I have left to live?" he asked in a trembling voice.

That's... dread, I explained to my heart as if I were teaching a class.

I sat down on the couch and leaned back.

"It's just that... I wish I would be granted just two more years of life," he said, looking up at me this time.

I held in my breath. *That's... hope*, I thought. I'd been going around the world teaching on that very topic for years. And here I was sitting with my own beloved who was uttering hope bitterly, and what was I to do?

"Suppose, Dad... suppose you have a couple more years, and I'm sure you do... what would you do with that time?"

He leaned forward slowly, interlacing his fingers and frowning a bit, as if he had a headache.

"I'd probably do things I always wanted to do but didn't get to do."

"Like what?"

"Like traveling with your mom."

"Oh. Where would you go with her?"

"Vienna... Paris... London... Cuba..."

"Wow, that's very specific. Why do you want to go to all those places?"

A faint smile emerged on his face, and he took a deep breath before attempting to speak.

"Well, I promised forty-eight years ago when she married me. I told her that we'd visit the graves of the greatest minds that ever lived. We need to pay them our tribute."

"Wow, that's amazing. What else would you like to do?" I asked.

He went on to tell me how he'd always wanted to be in the audience when I gave a lecture. He wanted to finish his book. He wanted to go back to Korea to say his goodbyes. That was all supposing he had a couple more years to go.

"I'll call it a tomb tour," he said, chuckling at his own morbid joke.

Much later that night, when I went downstairs to say goodnight, I found him searching something on his computer. I thought he was researching his diagnosis and prognosis. When I got close, I could see he was searching for last-minute flight deals. Later that same week, my parents left for Cuba and were gone for two weeks.

That's how Dad's battle with cancer began.

> **"**
>
> Behind every regret and fear lies a little wish. How do we hold on to that little wish to make a memory of the preferred future?
>
> **"**

Imagineer a preferred future

Behind every regret and fear lies a little wish. That's what I've learned from my conversations with people in despair. My work is to hold on to that hint of hope, and to grow it bigger by paying attention to it. I describe this as making the memory of your preferred future.

In such a conversation, you don't impose your preference or possibility on another. They compose their own preferred memory. You simply invite yourself to witness their supposed, not imposed, realities. As they imagine *what* could be, many ways of *how* to get there emerge—"imagineering" their preferred future.

Tina, a deeply caring young mother of two, came to talk to me about feeling inadequate as a parent. Early in our conversation, she said, "I don't ask for anything, I just want my kids to be happy with me."

"You want them to be happy with you," I reflected back, and then: "Suppose they are happy with you, what would be happening then?"

"We'll all relax and have fun together. We won't worry about things. The kids will stay with me. They won't get in trouble."

"Okay. So, suppose the kids stay with you and you all relax and have fun together. What difference would that make for you?"

"I won't feel like a horrible mother. And... hmm..."

"Okay, what would you feel like instead?"

"More like... a good mother." Tina paused, took a breath. "A good mother that they deserve."

"And when was the most recent time you felt like a good mother to them?" I asked.

"Uh... maybe last Saturday, a little bit. I read them a book before they fell asleep in my bed. We all slept in my bed together because I stayed home all night."

In a coaching conversation, you usually will get just a glimpse. Wishes show up so subtly, many times as an offshoot of a person's regrets and fears. The work is to attend to that delicate offshoot, so that it remains grafted and growing, as they weave their resourceful past through their preferred future.

Reflection Guide

One of the most useful ways to imagineer a preferred future in Solution-Focused brief coaching is a Miracle Question. Take your time answering the following prompts:

- Suppose, just suppose, somehow the changes that you hope to see in yourself or in your life begin to happen overnight while you are still sleeping, almost like a miracle... As you slowly wake up the next morning, what difference might you notice about you or around you?

- Please make a detailed list of twenty differences that you might notice about you or around you in that morning after the miracle.

- Who else might notice some of these differences throughout the day? How might they react to it?

- Suppose your miracle continues throughout the day. What difference would that make for the way you interact with others? What difference would that make for them?

- Thinking back over the last few days or weeks, what differences have already happened even in a small way?

Toward

Calibrate people's attention to move
toward the desired direction instead of
avoiding the unwanted direction.

a b c

d e f g h

i j k l m

n o p q r

s t u v w

x y z

I'M ONE OF those people who comes out of the mall and confidently walks in the wrong direction to find her car. My friends often tease that, for me, GPS stands for "God Please Save poor Haesun." When I was younger, before mobile phones and GPS, my lousy sense of direction sometimes got me into trouble. Such was the case one summer day when I was working as a camp counselor at an international school, a day when I also experienced a mysterious miracle I don't fully understand or quite believe even still.

I was assigned a bus full of children from Mexico, ages seven to fourteen. We had what should have been a fun itinerary—hiking along a section of Canada's famed Bruce Trail. The bus dropped us off in a parking lot at an entrance to the trail, and we were to meet back there in ninety minutes. I was handed a walkie-talkie in case anything went wrong.

"Just follow the white trail markers on the trees," the park ranger said. I stood studying the map on a big sign for a few minutes before the kids began nagging.

"Okay, okay, let's just go," I said to the group.

A quick-footed kid ran ahead of us, pointing at a tree and howling something in Spanish. He had spotted a trail marker. Good job. We followed those infrequent white markers down into the forest and improvised some turns when there was no more path ahead. The kids giggled whenever I tried saying something in Spanish. They taught me how to say "I love you" and "You are stupid" and "Be quiet." I learned that the quick-footed kid was Rafael; he was fluent in English, and he was joined by his younger sister, Martha. Suddenly, I noticed the terrain had become quite rough.

"*Cuidado!*" I said. *Watch out!* Some kids giggled, the oldest ones watching my face.

"Um ... do you see markers on any trees?" I asked.

We looked around. No markings. We stood on flat ground, but I saw a steep downward slope a few yards to our left. The area to the right seemed like a dead end with thick bushes taller than us. The older kids began to look concerned.

"Don't worry. No problem," I said, smiling as I switched on the walkie-talkie. It crackled, so I adjusted the frequency, but to no avail. A little one approached me with a frown.

"*Agua*," she said, and a few others soon joined her. It was so disorienting.

"*Silencio!*" I shouted. I paced back and forth as the kids became more exhausted by the minute. One by one, they sat on the ground. Rafael came up beside me and asked in a low voice if he could help.

"Rafael, how old are you?"

"Fourteen."

"Okay... and what ideas do you have?"

"I think we can go different ways and check."

"No, that's too dangerous. You'll get lost."

"No, we just go straight for three minutes and come back. Teamwork," he explained, giving me a thumbs-up. It was growing darker and I was out of options.

"Okay, just for three minutes."

Rafael quickly organized a few teams of older kids to scout the nearby terrain.

Working with the
presence of goals
is much easier than
contending with the
absence of goals.

"Please come back if it looks too dangerous," I said. "And turn around immediately after three minutes."

"No problem," one of the other kids said, winking at me. They went off in three different directions.

"Can you hear me?" I hollered when the teams disappeared from my sight. They hollered back. The light was fading, and I panicked when none of them hollered back at my most recent call. Every possible worst-case scenario passed through my head.

Martha crawled to my side, and I tried comforting her. After the longest six minutes ever, Rafael popped out of the thicket.

"Oh God, you're back!" I said, relieved.

Martha burst out crying. One by one, they all came back, but not with good news. At our left, I was told, was a sheer drop down to what seemed to be a fast stream. To our right through the thicket was a natural wilderness, unexplored, they knew, because they had come across a giant, intact spider web. The last kids to return said they had seen no markers or clear paths. As Rafael reported all this to me, the boys updated the little ones in Spanish, and a few of them began to cry. I'd never before in my life felt so desperate. I told the kids to sit down and, after they settled, asked if they knew how to pray. Most raised their hands.

"Let's pray. Please pray," I said.

I saw them make the sign of the cross and close their eyes as they started praying together in Spanish. It sounded like the Lord's Prayer. I closed my eyes and prayed aloud.

"God, please help us. Don't leave us here. Send your rescue."

I said amen and all the kids did, too. When we opened our eyes, we saw the bushes to our right rustle. I jumped back and we all screamed. A young man dressed in walking shorts and a white T-shirt suddenly appeared. He didn't look surprised to see us. He smiled at me.

"Hey, are you lost?" he asked.

"Yes! Yes! Please get us out of here!"

I was beyond glad to see another adult.

He gestured for us to follow him as he headed in the direction of the sheer drop.

"No. There's no way out there," I told him as I followed a few steps behind.

"Come and see," he said.

As we turned the corner, we saw a staircase leading up out of the forest. A staircase. In the middle of nowhere, there was a staircase. The kids had already passed through here scouting, where there was, unmistakably, a staircase winding up.

"Go ahead," he urged.

We all ran, not knowing where we would end up. As I climbed the last few steps out of the woods, I saw that it was still broad daylight. I couldn't believe it. It was the very parking lot where we were supposed to meet the driver. It was so disorienting. I saw our bus. The driver spotted us and waved his hand like there was no rush. When I turned around to say thank you, the young man was gone.

Pay attention to approaching, not avoiding

In the first session of a coaching class, I usually use the analogy of an airport taxi driver and his passenger. Let's say you just disembarked from the plane at an airport in a country you're not familiar with, and you climb into a taxi. You may exchange some quick pleasantries with the driver, but the most important exchange begins with, "Where to?" It would be strange if the driver asked where you had come from before asking where you were going. Now, let's suppose the driver poses his question and the passenger gives an unexpected response:

"Where to?"
"Away. Away from this airport, please."

That response is absurd, and the driver would likely suspect the passenger is a fugitive of some kind. If I were the driver, I'd ask the passenger to leave my car, or else I'd leave the vehicle!

Coaching conversations, or conversations concerned with people making positive changes, should begin with, "Where to?" But the tendency is to start with, "Where from?" Perhaps this happens because of the habit of asking, "What's wrong?" so that we can help others fix the problem. Many coaches also bring the habits from their previous profession as counselor, psychologist, physician, human resource practitioner, social worker, or even therapist: identify the root cause, diagnose, and prescribe to treat. The most popular "Where from?" sounds like this: "What brings you in today?"

How would you answer that? One person may say, "I've been struggling with something and I don't want to continue it. I want to make it stop"— whatever "it" might be. For some, it's an addiction. For others, it's unwanted relationships or interactions or other situations they perceive to be unfavorable. It's an away-from-the-airport answer. How do you help people orient their attention to "Where to?" Here's one example from my conversation with Gerry:

> **Haesun:** Gerry, thanks for coming in. So, after our conversation today, as you get back to your life, what will tell you that things are moving forward to where you want them to be?
>
> **Gerry:** Well, if I don't have to deal with incompetent people on my project team, that'd be a relief. In fact, this whole project, if I can just delegate it away. That's what gives me the most stress.
>
> **Haesun:** Okay. You don't want to be stressed about it.
>
> **Gerry:** Right. If this constant stress could just stop.

So far, Gerry was focused on what's called *avoidance goals*—wanting the absence of something. He wanted to move away from the unpleasant circumstances of incompetent people. Typically, with New Year's resolutions, people set avoidance goals—stop smoking, lose weight, stop wasting resources like money or time. The follow-through rate for such resolutions is often close to zero.

"And suppose it [the constant stress] stops, what would be there instead of stress?"

When I continued the conversation with Gerry, he responded with, "Rest. My head will rest. No more project planning and all that, just be quiet. No stress, just more room for everyone to joke around and enjoy each other."

Do you see the where-to answer there? Gerry was clearer about what he didn't want earlier, but now he moves toward what he wants. This is what's called *approach goals*—wanting the presence of something. Working with the presence of goals is much easier than contending with the absence of goals.

"So you want your head to be quiet, and you want more room for everyone to enjoy each other."

Gerry smiled and nodded. "Yes, exactly."

Compared with what Gerry said at the beginning ("I don't want to deal with incompetent people on my project team, and I want to delegate the whole project"), Gerry's response shows a drastic change: "I want more room for everyone to enjoy each other." How does this shift happen? Gerry simply oriented from what he wanted to avoid to what he wanted to approach.

Reflection Guide

We make thousands of small and big decisions—what to eat, what to wear, what to say—throughout the day. Deciding on one thing actively eliminates other options. When we choose what to eat, for example, we are also deciding what not to eat. Consider many of your choices from the past week:

- What small but significant decisions brought you closer to what you care about?

- What decision should be made soon, so that it may serve you and people around you well?

- What are some of your own avoidance goals (what not to do) that you'd like to shift to approach goals (what to do)?

Useful

Filter their experiences through the lens of
how the experiences came to be and how they
could be helpful for desired changes.

a b c
d e f g h
i j k l m
n o p q r
s t **u** v w
x y z

AROUND THE LONG WEEKEND in May, Dad would begin to carry with him a small wallet whenever he went out for a walk. On days when he didn't return within thirty minutes, we knew what he was up to—rummaging through a neighborhood garage sale. He brought home knick-knacks like old-fashioned bottle openers and manual air pumps. There were some good finds, too, like an artist's original painting and a bicycle, which are both still in use today. One weekend when I was home from university for the summer, Dad went for his walk and returned in less than fifteen minutes.

"Oh, you're back early, Dad."

He grinned, eagerly grabbed his car keys and work gloves, and prepared to leave again.

"Where're you going?" I asked.

He was elated, like a kid with a new toy.

"Oh, I gotta go pick up something, just down the street. Wanna come?"

I decided to tag along. Just two blocks down, I saw a yellow bristol board sign that read "Garage Sale" tied to a tree. Several cars were parked by the curb, and a dozen people were hunting through piles of paraphernalia.

"What did you get?" I asked.

Beaming with satisfaction, he gestured for me to follow him, and we traversed the driveway-turned-market. Still wondering, I looked around to guess at his purchase. This loveseat? That coffee table? *Oh, look at that miter saw.* We made our way past the side of the house to the backyard.

"Dad, I don't think we should go back there," I said, grasping his arm.

"Look!" he said, placing his hand on mine where I was holding his arm. He pointed to a stack of five huge tree stumps. Attached to one was a Post-it note that read "Sold to Moons." That was us. The tree stumps were ours.

"These?" I said, flabbergasted.

"Yeah, help me carry them," he said and handed me his work gloves to put on.

"We have a gas fireplace. You know that, right?" I commented sarcastically as he handed me an armful, rough bark scoring my shirt.

"These are not firewood," he chuckled.

"Excuse me! Coming through!" he called out as we made our way back and forth until we had moved all five stumps. Embarrassed, I sneered at him.

"You know, these are actually trash, not treasure."

"You'll see," he said, looking at me over his glasses and smiling.

For the next few weeks, we were not allowed in his garage while he worked on his surprise project. We occasionally heard power tools grunting along with him, but his tired, cheerful face showed up every night at dinner.

Then one sunny day before their wedding anniversary, Dad took Mom's hand, and he ushered her to the backyard. He asked all three of us children to attend the grand unveiling, too. A tarp covered a small mound in the backyard. He must have installed it early in the morning.

"Ready?" he said.

He gave one corner of the tarp to Mom and gestured for her to lift it. As she carefully tugged on the cover, a beautiful set of five wood stools appeared. He had carved many facets into each, making them look like jewels. They were stained ash brown and had been treated for outdoor use. Each stool had an M engraved into it. We stood speechless as Dad embraced Mom.

"Happy twenty-fifth, my love."

Even the past is malleable

A lot of people come in for coaching through a program for alumni at the University of Toronto. Through this program, I have met many delightful moms who wanted to return to the workforce after mothering for a few years before their child reached school age. Jamie was one of them. She had worked as a professional photographer for nearly two decades before she got married. She'd moved to a new city and had two boys. By the time her youngest reached five, she had been a full-time stay-at-home partner for ten years.

"It feels like I'm starting from scratch," she said. "It's hard. When I was working as a photographer, we didn't have digital photography. I worked with

35-millimeter film and had my own darkroom. Now, everyone's a photographer. It's like the rest of the world moved on while I've been stuck with kids, wasting the past ten years," she said. "Don't get me wrong," she quickly added. "I love them to bits and I'd do it all over again."

"So, what are some useful things you learned in the past ten years that you didn't know before?" I asked.

"Oh my gosh, are you kidding? When you become a mother, you become a doctor, nurse, teacher, cleaner, chef, secretary all at once! I wish I had known how to manage so many balls up in the air when I was working as a solo artist."

"Ha, okay. Now, having learned to do that, what difference do you think it might make when you get back to being an artist?"

"Well, I wasn't earning money, but I don't think I left my art while I was raising kids."

"Oh, okay. In what ways did you keep your art alive in your life?"

"In the last nine months, as I was anticipating getting back to work again, I taught myself a few digital media like documentary making."

Even our past
is malleable.

"Wow, how did you manage to make the time with two kids and all?"

"See, you really get good at managing so many balls in the air as a mom. This was one of those important balls I didn't want to drop. So, I kept it up there."

By the end of our forty-five-minute conversation, Jamie said she was probably readier than before to succeed as a solo visual artist in the marketplace. She had learned so many useful skills being a mother, and she was grateful to have a useful pause in her career so that she could get back to it more strongly than ever before.

Did you hear that? From "wasted time" to a "useful career pause." It made my day to hear her say that. Now, how did that change come about?

When you sit with another in conversation listening into their past, you may hear the difficulties, disappointments, or even disasters. Yet knowing that they are past gives tremendous hope. Your next curiosity can be focused on how they coped with those experiences, what they learned from them, and how they are making the best use of them. You will witness something transforming right in front of your eyes. Try it. It will make your day.

Reflection Guide

You might have experienced some pauses in your life—
because of being a parent or a caregiver, or because of
an illness, a loss, a pandemic, accidents, or even getting into or out of a relationship.

- How have you coped with a pause? Who or what
  supported you through?

- What did you learn from the pause that made you
  who you are today?

- What do you now know about yourself—your values and boundaries—that you didn't know then?

Value

Evoke deeper meaning and a sense of
worth in and through story-listening.

"JENNIE, CAN YOU help me with something in my office after class?"

That's what they called me: Jennie. Moving to Toronto at the age of seventeen wasn't easy. It meant a new school in a new country. My name was considered "ethnic" in Canada and people had a hard time pronouncing it. They tried, though: *Hey-Soon, Hi-Sheen, Hu-Sein*. I'm not sure what made it so difficult when the name was spelled phonetically in English for their sake: *Hae-sun*. I remember my grade eleven homeroom teacher doing the roll call on my first day of school.

"Daniel?"

"Here."

"Elizabeth?"

"Yes."

"Frank?"

"Here."

Then he stopped to lift his head slightly to adjust the angle at which he looked through his bifocals and cleared his throat.

"Um ... Moon? Where is Moon?" he asked, looking around the room.

Some kids snickered. Who names their kid Moon? I wasn't sure if he meant me since he had called the other kids by their first names, so I didn't say anything. He looked down at his attendance sheet again and gave it another try.

"Hey ... How ... Soon ... Moon?"

Okay, that sounds more like me, I thought, so I raised my hand (and the giggles grew).

"Oh, there you are," he said in a genuinely welcoming tone and smiling. "Okay, your name is too difficult to pronounce. Um, so, say what ... how about Jennie? That's my daughter's name. Jennie. Do you like that?"

Before you get livid at this inappropriate response, let me say that this was not an unusual practice at the time. He was probably just trying to be helpful to a kid who had left all her friends behind in another land and now found herself in Canada, where she didn't speak much of the language. Before I learned to speak English, I learned to nod politely, pretending to understand what was being said. I wasn't sure what the teacher had just said, but I didn't know how to tell him that and ask him to clarify.

"Uhum..." I said, nodding. And that's how my new name got registered on my school record, for all my classes.

I did well in the classes where they used universal symbols, like math and chemistry. The physics teacher was fun, so I showed up every time. History and biology were nightmares. I didn't know what they were teaching in class. My new school didn't even use the world map that I was used to in Korea! My frustration only grew in the coming weeks. I couldn't express that frustration in words well yet, and I began hanging out with some rough kids who smoked and skipped classes. It was on just such a day that I arrived at physics class reeking of cigarette smoke.

"Jennie, can you help me with something in my office after class?" Mr. Caruna asked. He always wore a friendly facial expression that made it look like he was about to tell a joke.

"Yes," I said in my limited vocabulary, shrugging my shoulders.

After class, he asked me to help him carry some props back to his office. As we walked together, he casually asked if I liked physics. I said yes, and he said how impressed he had been with my most recent assignment, building a catapult, adding that it must have taken a lot of time. We put the props down on his desk and he turned to me.

"Jennie, I know you are hanging out with some people. You are very smart, and you know that's not the best choice. I can really see that you have so much potential, and you need to make good decisions about your friends."

I just stood there looking somewhat aloof.

"And Jennie, it took me a while to find yours," he said, pointing at my catapult, "because you signed it HM. What does that stand for?"

"Uh . . . Haesun Moon. My name."

"Haesun. That's a beautiful name. Does it have a meaning?"

"Yes, it does. It means *give grace*."

Venting is often our values in disguise

"So, what would you like to see change or continue at work?"

Yoshi was the founder and owner of a café franchise. When he called it a passion project, his zeal for work shone through his mild demeanor. He had started with a small coffee shop near a university campus, and it had become a local favorite, with a few franchise cafés. His business grew rapidly. So, too, did his frustration with a few franchisees over inventory management.

"I really want the franchisees to follow the shelf-life policy for baked goods," he said.

Depending on the kind of baked goods, the ideal shelf life could be anywhere from four to eight hours. Each franchisee signed off on the policy, yet during his spot checks at the cafés, Yoshi had noticed that the policy was often disregarded. He understood that franchisees were trying to maximize profit, but it compromised the quality. Yoshi called the shelf-life policy their linchpin.

"What is it about this shelf-life policy that's so important to you?" I asked in one coaching session.

Story-listening is a highly
evocative activity for both the
narrator and the listener.
As you sit with the other in
the stories told, what you
listen to evokes values.

"It's not just a policy. It's a promise to our customers."

"A promise? What does it promise?"

"A promise that they are getting something fresh, each and every time. Good food they can trust." Yoshi emphasized that last part.

"It's a promise of good food," I repeated back.

"Yes, and if we compromise that, there's nothing left of us." At this point, Yoshi's resolute look softens to a sudden smile. "I know exactly what to do. I'm gonna call the policy 'A Good Food Promise' from now on!"

Story-listening is a highly evocative activity for both the narrator and the listener. As you sit with the other in the stories told, what you listen to evokes values: what they think is worth telling and what you think is worth hearing. In that space, you choose what to listen for. There are stories about why they want something different to begin with (purpose), how they'd rather have it (preference), what may become available as a result of that change (possibilities), and what's already working in that direction (progress). When you are listening for those stories of purpose, preference, possibilities, and progress, the simple story of a broken policy becomes a monumental milestone in the making of a promise. Behind every vent is a value.

Reflection Guide

Every family or group of people that comes together has formal and informal rules. These can be as mundane as who's taking the trash out, or they could be deep-seated patterns of interactions and taboo topics.

- What are some of the rules in your household, especially the unspoken ones that a visitor may even find strange?

- What rules or policies do people around you often complain about?

- Reflecting back on some of those rules and policies, what are they intending to promise or protect?

Wonder

Respectfully and tentatively suggest alternate interpretations or actions for consideration.

"SO, WHAT ARE you gonna try out in your life after you leave this class?" is how I often finished the first day of a coaching class. Students have insights or ideas to implement in their life right away, and getting them to articulate that is an important part of learning. But that day, I was hesitant to ask the question because one participant didn't seem too engaged. He'd sat through the entire day without saying much or even taking notes, and I wondered if he was getting anything useful out of the class. But I asked anyway and, to my surprise, he put up his hand.

"Yes, Al?"

"Well, I went out during lunch and bought this," he said, pulling out what looked like a marker.

"You got a marker…"

"Yeah. It's a dry erase marker."

"Okay. And what is your idea with it?"

"I'm gonna put positive messages for my daughter on the bathroom mirror at home."

The entire class responded affectionately to this unexpectedly sweet gesture, and I was rather relieved.

"Okay, Al, that sounds quite fun. Will you please share with us how that goes?"

Throughout the entire week before the next class, I wondered how Al's experiment was going. When I walked into the classroom the following week, I saw Al surrounded by a few other students. They were all laughing together.

"Good morning!" I said, making eye contact with Al, who had a wide grin. More students trickled in behind me. Within a few minutes, we were all settled in our seats.

"So, what's been better, clearer, different since our last class?" I asked. That's often how I start a second class. Al put up his hand, blushing slightly.

"Yes, Al?"

He told us about his experiment at home with the marker. As soon as he'd arrived at home, he'd written a message on the bathroom mirror: "Taylor, you

have a big, kind heart. Daddy loves you." He'd encir-
cled these words of affection in a large heart.

The next morning, Al and his wife heard their
daughter wake up, visit the bathroom, and then run
downstairs right away. She gave Al a big hug and said,
"I love you, Daddy."

The next morning Al went into the bathroom and
found a message from Taylor: "You are the best dad
in the whole world. I love you. Have a good day." She
had drawn many small hearts all around the message.
That was their new morning surprise to each other.

The entire class responded with, "Aww…"

"And that's not all," Al said, beaming with big,
ingenuous eyes. After his experiment at home, he'd
felt inspired to try something like that at work. He
managed a restaurant and had about forty regular
staff members. He'd brought his marker to work the
next day. Before anyone else arrived, he'd written on
the mirror in the staff-only washroom, "You guys
always make my day better. Thank you for being
awesome."

Later, Al was waiting in anticipation for people
to notice and react. To his slight disappointment, no
one said anything. Quite confused, Al went into the

washroom that night. Yes, the message was still there, but no one had talked to him about it! He added a couple more positive messages in a more prominent place. The next day, staff members arrived and used the washroom numerous times, but still no one seemed to notice. Perplexed, Al decided to do it once more the following morning. By now, he'd grown a bit skeptical about his idea. Maybe people didn't care after all. This time, he left personalized thank-you messages to staff members who were working that day. Again, no one seemed to notice it or care.

"Oh, I felt so dejected, almost getting angry," he told us. The class was anxious as we listened to the tale of his disheartening experiment at work. How ungrateful these people were!

"But then the next morning, I went into work a bit later than usual. I felt something was off, unsettled. Apparently, an overnight cleaner had wiped the mirror clean. All the staff members were livid and came to me saying how upsetting it was that the messages were gone. They had all been reading them, apparently!"

The whole class laughed and applauded in relief and with satisfaction. He said the team members had started writing messages to each other, too, and some of them even decided to do so in the public washroom for the customers! What a story, and all this in one week. We all celebrated the story. After we took turns sharing similar stories in class, it was already time for our first break. Some went off to get coffee and snacks, and I went to the washroom. As I turned to the sink to wash my hands, I saw it: almost like a miracle, an uplifting message and a big heart on the mirror looking right at me.

The art of advice is understanding another's life logic first

How often do you have an apt opportunity for offering advice? It might be someone younger than you, newer than you to certain life experiences, or "under" you in an organizational hierarchy. ("Been there, done that, and here's my advice…") Most people genuinely mean well and justify advice-giving by saying, "I just don't want you to learn the lesson the hard way."

"You really should sleep-train your baby," the parent of a toddler says to the parent of a newborn.

" Your own logic, the
way you understand
and organize your
world, may get in the
way of inquiring about
the other's logic. "

"Follow your dream, be the best you can be," a motivational speaker tells a teenager struggling at home.

"Take time to take care of yourself first," a corporate trainer says to a group of essential workers during a pandemic.

Suggestions like these often elicit the response, "Yes, but..."

"Yes, but I don't want my baby to think I don't care. She's different than yours," the new parent objects.

"Yes, but my family brings out the worst in me. You don't live at my house," the irate teenager cries.

"Yes, but people are dying right in front of us. You haven't seen those faces," the exhausted nurses demur.

When you sit in conversation with someone, consider them to be experts at doing their own lives.

In coaching conversations, you are called simply to witness and wonder about how another person does their living—what is their *logic* for their life? Your own logic, the way you understand and organize your world, may get in the way of inquiring about their logic. If you don't try to understand their logic, your advice is, at best, a far-fetched suggestion or an irrelevant opinion. I'm not discounting the value that you may add to another person's logic—I'm simply wondering about the best ways to do that.

What if you approached your own advice by wondering if it may offer any value to the other?

"Not getting enough sleep is so tough. You might have already been doing something about this, but I wonder if you might consider sleep training for your child."

What do you imagine the first-time parent would say to this?

"I don't know what struggles you may have, but I assume that you're hoping to somehow follow your dream. I wonder if you'd consider what that looks like when you are showing up the way that you truly want, even in those struggles?"

How do you think the teenager would respond to this wonderment?

"I can't even imagine what it's like to work the front lines of a pandemic, and I'm wondering what you're doing to cope with all this, because you are clearly taking care of yourself as best you can, given the situation."

What aspects of their lives would the nurses think about? What they're doing right (their resources) or what they're not doing right (their deficits)? The next time you feel inclined to offer advice, I wonder if you'd pause and connect to your sense of wonder about the other. What strength are they bringing to their current circumstances? How might you weave in your acknowledgment of that? How might you witness the resources they bring to bear while wondering if and how your perspective might add?

Reflection Guide

Technological advances sometimes get in the way of sensing wonder. Before we pause to wonder, we ask Google, Siri, or Alexa. They quench the questions that we didn't even know we had. The noise of the virtual world scatters our attention far too easily. Here are some activities for you to consider to enhance your sense of wonder:

- What are some of your routines and rituals (first in the morning or last before bed) that seem to anchor you?

- Look around where you are right now. What do you see? What is it made of? How does it work? If it could talk, what would it complain about? What advice would it have for you?

- Suppose a small but pleasant surprise awaits you tomorrow, what would it be? How would you respond to that surprise?

X on a Scale

Use a scale as a metaphor of a person's growth and progress.

a b c
d e f g h
i j k l m
n o p q r
s t u v w
x y z

YOU MIGHT HAVE experienced it—renovating a house. It can quickly become a bigger, messier, and lengthier project than what you started out thinking. Mine did. It started with just wanting to replace a sink in the bathroom. This bathroom hadn't been touched in years, for as long as I could remember.

The toilet, tub, and sink all matched in hippie-sixties baby pink, and the brown and gold linoleum had started to curl up in the corners. When my dad and my brother and I scraped off the golden-butterfly wallpaper, we found pencil writing on the walls. The first thing we saw was "Jim R., 1964." When we removed the mirror that covered almost half the wall, we found numbers, seemingly measurements made when positioning the mirror and lights. The mirror had a date stamp on the back, along with a

"Made in West Germany" mark on it. West Germany. That had to go back quite some time, too. When we were removing the last bit of wallpaper by the door, we found a previously painted wall with markings at chest level: "Terry—77/10/11," with an inch-long line beside it, and "Jimmy—78/5/3," with another line below. We saw still more when we scraped off the final strip of paper: "Terry—76/12/23," "Jimmy—77/12/23," and similar patterns continuing downward and backward through time.

"Oh, it's a growth chart!" Dad said. "Terry and Jimmy were their names!"

He put down his scraper and crouched on one knee by the wall. He took his glove off and ran his hand over the markings as if he were caressing the foreheads of the children standing there for their dad to measure them. The image of Jim, whom we never met, measuring the increasing heights of his growing sons brought a smile to Dad's face. And my memory of Dad's discovery still tugs at my heart today.

"

The X on the scale
is a metaphor of
progress—not of
progress that needs
to be made, but
progress that has
been made so far.

"

Every point on a scale is a sign of progress

Remember the ten-to-one scale? I often ask my clients a variation of this question: "On a scale of ten to one, where ten is where you feel that you're good enough and quite content with your life and one is the opposite, where do you think you are at right now?" I sometimes draw the scale with a marker on a whiteboard. Sometimes I use masking tape on the floor. And I ask them to mark X with a marker on the whiteboard or simply walk toward that spot on their scale. The choice is theirs and it can be any number between one and ten. What follows their choice is my choice of curiosity. What am I curious about?

"I'd say I'm here right now," Mahmood said, stopping at about what would be the number two point on the floor scale.

"All right, about here," I said, moving a half-step and stopping beside him.

"Yes, I've got a long way to go," he said, pointing with his chin over to the ten position.

"Right. And as you look back at the one..." I said. I gestured for him to look to the other end of the scale.

"Yeah, that's about two months ago," he said.

"And what got you to here from where you were just two months ago?"

"Well, I've made some major changes in my schedule, so I can have one day a week protected as my family time."

"And what positive differences have you been noticing in the last while as you've made this change and protected your family time?"

"Oh, huge," he said, and grinned. "I mean, I'm so much more effective at work knowing that I'll have one day less to work."

We both laughed.

"And the kids love that I'm there with them without checking my phone or computer every two minutes." He went on to tell me about some other changes he'd noticed in his relationship with his partner, with their two children, and even his relationships at work. "Actually, I'm gonna put myself a bit higher than this," he said, chuckling and stepping forward on the scale. I followed.

At this point in such a conversation, I often remember the bathroom growth chart. Wouldn't it be absurd if someone used a growth chart to mark their *future* growth? How tall are you planning to be by next month? Next year? It would be odd to say to your children, "Here's the line you ought to reach by next October. Let's work on it!" Yet, in conversations with others, we sometimes make that common but unusual leap of future growth. The markings on the growth chart are always about measuring the height that has been reached at the time of recording. "How did you manage to get up to this point [X] already?" is a very different invitation than, "How will you manage to get up to that point?" The X on the scale is a metaphor of progress—not of progress that needs to be made, but progress that has been made so far.

Reflection Guide

Here are some useful scaling exercises for your own reflection. Feel free to use this space to mark your X, or get a pen and paper to write on.

- Look at some of these aspects of your life on a scale of ten to one. Some areas may resonate with you more strongly than others. Ten (10) is where you feel you've reached your full growth potential, and one (1) is the sorry opposite of that. Place an X somewhere along each of these scales:

  Physical Growth   1 _____10

  Emotional Growth   1 _____10

  Financial Growth   1 _____10

  Intellectual Growth 1 _____10

  Relational Growth   1 _____10

  Spiritual Growth   1 _____10

  Vocational Growth   1 _____10

- Select two areas that you'd like to explore further. As you look at the Xs on these two scales, how did you manage to arrive at those numbers and not lower ones? (If you said one, how are you coping as well as you are there?) List at least ten responses.

- How do the two areas relate to one another? How does one influence the other?

- What ideas and insights do you have now after reflecting on this?

Yet

Encourage anticipation of progress.

---

a b c
d e f g h
i j k l m
n o p q r
s t u v w
x y z

HAVE YOU EVER waited for someone to arrive at the airport?

Some hold flowers, others hold "Welcome" placards. People pace back and forth around the gate, checking the flight arrival times. Every time the opaque gates slide open, everyone turns, making whoever comes through the gate feel like a celebrity. The nature of some encounters seems obvious. Someone holds up a name card for a man just arriving. A handshake. Probably a business trip. A young woman arrives with a small suitcase and coyly looks through the crowd...

"Laura!" shouted a young man running with flowers. Then a kiss, rather passionate for an airport. Probably Laura's lover. We rubberneckers chuckled. A cart stacked high with bound suitcases and taped boxes wheeled out through the gates. We onlookers could barely see the hat of the porter pushing it. It bumped slightly as it crossed the threshold, and the load leaned to one side. A few of us gasped, and someone mumbled, "*Somebody's* moving." Two men approached the cart, and the face of a petite elderly woman behind the porter lit up. She held her hands up to grab the face of the younger of the two. Kisses on both cheeks. Probably a grandma and her grandson. We onlookers shaped stories in our imaginations about the passing encounters.

The gates opened again and a man in a military uniform carrying an oversized backpack strode across the threshold. The waiting hall quieted momentarily.

"Papa!" we heard a child's voice call out, and our eyes traced the little one running toward his father. He slowed down his steps, and a big smile emerged on his face. The man bent to his knees and stretched out his hands.

"Papa! Papa!" the little one shouted, hopping into his father's arms.

How satisfying for all of us to see that reunion. We onlookers grinned and "awwed" to ourselves. We couldn't look away just yet as the man's eyes scanned the crowd for the grown-up who must have been accompanying the child. He spotted her, and we did, too. He stood up straight, still holding the child's hand. She walked dramatically toward the soldier. Soon they were standing close enough to hear each other. They looked at each other without saying anything, searching each other's faces. Would there be a hug? Was she crying? Where had he been? Curiosity held our attention as the man stretched out his free hand to caress the woman's face. She raised her arm and wrapped his hand in hers. They said something but we couldn't hear what. Then they hugged, not a brief, friendly hug, but a deep, long embrace that said, *It's really you. It's really me.* The little one held on to their legs and buried his head between them. I don't know who started it, but now we were all clapping. The soldier gave us all a brief wave before the family made their way out of the crowd. I wondered what stories they would share with each other that night.

Take "I don't know" as "I don't know *yet*"

Seventeen-year-old Riley walked into my office forty minutes late to his fifty-five-minute appointment. I had met him briefly for the first time about a week before when he'd come with his mother to book this appointment.

"Hey, Riley! You made it."

"Yeah," he said as he stood in the doorway, his backpack drooping to one side.

"Come in and sit down," I said as I got up to move to the consulting table. He plopped down on the chair in front of me, still with his hoodie covering his head.

"So, Riley, you came straight from school or what?"

"Yeah."

"Okay, so how do you want to use the time that we have?"

He shrugged. "I don't know," he mumbled.

"Okay, so you don't know yet."

"Uh-huh."

"So, do you want to take some time to think about it or do you already have some ideas?"

He inhaled sharply. "Like, I don't want nobody to be on my case."

"What do you mean?"

"Like, Mom sent me here, right?"

"Right."

"She's just gotta chill, I already stopped doing some stuff that I was doing before."

"You did?"

"Uh-huh."

"And she doesn't know that yet?"

"No. That's my business. Nobody needs to know that."

"Okay, so you want Mom to chill and not get on your case."

"See, I'm not a child," he said, rolling his eyes. "She needs to know that I'm an adult."

"Okay. She doesn't know that you're an adult yet."

"No, she doesn't."

"So... what do you think will help her know that you're an adult?"

He seemed reluctant to say it, but the question led Riley to see that he had to help her know that he was making healthier decisions than before. He hadn't yet told her of his decision to focus more on school this year. He hadn't told her that he'd stopped doing drugs. In fact, he had started looking for a part-time job to save up for his first car, and she didn't know that yet. Before he left our fifteen-minute conversation, he mentioned that he would see how he could communicate with his mom better.

"See you next week," Riley said as he left my office.

Conversations can position your conversation partner to be their own witnesses. People can watch their own arrival at their preferred destinations.

"Okay, Riley," I said, smiling, because he didn't yet have another appointment booked, and thinking he'd be all right.

Conversations can position your conversation partner to be their own witnesses. People can watch their own arrival at their preferred destinations.

People are always trying to help themselves in one way or another. What happens in a conversation when you wait in anticipation for another person's resources and strengths to show up? When these qualities arrive, can you gently coax the other to pay closer attention to what's happening and to what stories are emerging for them? Stories await in our anticipation of their arrival, so all you need to do is simply wait for them.

Reflection Guide

The word "yet" creates room for anticipation.

- What are some of your examples of what is yet to come?

- What have you always wanted to learn that you have not learned yet?

- Think of someone you've known for a very long time that you care about. What hopes do you have for them that they may not have for themselves yet?

- What are some areas of your life where you are actively growing? Who are you becoming?

Zero

Focus on the presence of possibilities,
not absence of progress, even at
the lowest point on a scale.

RAISING CHILDREN ISN'T always easy. I mean, was it ever? When the COVID-19 pandemic hit, my now-teenaged nephews moved in with me for a while because their parents worked in essential services. I was living with Mom after Dad passed, and we welcomed the boys joining this rather empty house. I thought it would give Mom a useful distraction, and I thought, *How hard could it be?* Ha.

At first, the kids stayed home 24/7 doing virtual school. I stayed home 24/7 teaching online classes. Adjusting to each other's rhythms took much longer than we'd ever imagined. And the toughest part was learning to communicate with each other. They had this strange habit of answering all my questions with the word "nothing."

"Hey, why don't you fix yourself some breakfast?" I asked.

"There's *nothing* to eat," my nephew Jeremy said, grumpily closing the door of a fridge full of fresh produce and a variety of ingredients. Milk, yogurt, butter, jam, toastable waffles. *Oh, c'mon.*

"Hey, you're so underdressed for the weather," I said to Nathan on his way out in the middle of winter.

"There's *nothing* to wear," he said, shrugging it away and leaving the house with no scarf, no hat, no mittens. Seriously? Had he not seen the drawer downstairs?

"Hey, you guys, why are you sleeping in till noon?" I sometimes liked to ask on weekends.

"There's *nothing* to do," they would say in unison, as if they'd rehearsed their response.

"Yeah? Have you seen your rooms? They could use a bit of cleaning. Did you finish your homework? It's so sunny out, get outside!"

I often complained to Mom about the apparent lack of motivation or interest in these growing teenagers. She just smiled and listened. One day when I was complaining to Mom about exactly that, Jeremy walked into the kitchen rubbing his sleepy eyes. It was way past noon, and I gave him a disapproving look.

"Hello, young prince. Get enough sleep yet?" Mom asked cheerfully.

"Oh, good morning, Grandma," he lazily mumbled through his yawn as he reached for the fridge door.

"You mean good afternoon," I interjected.

No reply.

"Planning to make something?" Mom asked as Jeremy stared at the full fridge, with both doors wide open, as if there were nothing in it.

"Yeah, maybe." He grabbed a couple of eggs and some waffles, probably because they were in front of everything else.

"How are you cooking the eggs?" Mom asked.

Oh, please, he probably doesn't even know how to turn on the gas stove.

"Um…" he said, placing the eggs beside the stove.

"Because if you're gonna boil them, I'd love one, too."

That was odd, because she'd had her brunch not even an hour ago.

"Sure," he said like it was no big deal. "You want one too?" he asked me.

I was quite full, but I did not want to say no. As I was thinking about it, Mom chimed in.

"How nice! You are cooking for us!" Mom encouraged him as he filled a pot with water.

I was about to get up to turn on the stove for him, but Mom gently placed her hand on my lap. Jeremy grabbed a couple more eggs and put them all in the pot. He turned on the stove so naturally it was like he had been doing it every day. Not only that, he put a pinch of salt and even a capful of vinegar in the pot.

What? That's the trick that Mom taught me when I was little, so the shells don't break. How does he know that?

"Wow, you know to do that, too?" Mom said, sounding genuinely impressed. (So was I, actually.)

"Yeah, I saw both of you do it before," he said nonchalantly as he placed two waffles in the toaster.

"I'm so glad that you know how to make breakfast for yourself," I interjected cheerfully. "Breakfast is the most important meal of the day!"

"Um . . . it's afternoon, Auntie. It's lunch," Jeremy corrected me as he turned the dial on the egg timer. "How soft do you want your eggs to be done?"

Assume the presence of progress

I've heard many tales of Insoo Kim Berg and Steve de Shazer—the founders of the Solution-Focused approach to coaching—publicly talking through their different perspectives on the practice. For example, Steve liked using the scaling question phrased this way:

Practitioner: So, on a *scale of zero to ten*, where would you say that you are at right now?

Client: Uh... probably at zero today.

Practitioner: You're having it pretty tough today, huh?

Client: Yeah.

Practitioner: So, how do you cope with that... when things get tough like this? I mean, how did you even manage to come here?

Insoo's scaling question sounded subtly different. It is said that she wanted to assume some presence of client progress. So, she used a slightly different boundary:

People realize that
they are much closer to
what they want than they
thought—a process called
resource activation, or what
I'd call *ordinary magic*.

Practitioner: So, on a *scale of one to ten*, where would you say you are at?

Client: Probably a... one. One or two.

Practitioner: One or two. Wow, it's been pretty tough for you.

Client: Yeah.

Practitioner: But somehow you keep at it. You don't give up.

Client: No, I don't.

Practitioner: So, what keeps you going? How come you are not at zero, but are at a one or two already?

These are hypothetical examples for illustrative purposes, but what did you notice was different in the above examples? What was similar in what these two brilliant practitioners did? Whether the low end of the scale is set at zero or one, the practitioners persistently inquire about the presence of progress, rather than about the absence of it. In our ordinary conversations with our friends, family, and colleagues, we may hear them lament about having "zero" motivation, "no" idea, "not enough" money, or even "lack" of opportunities. It sounds like the absence of something at first, but what do you hear that they seem to care about, and what is present despite the perceived lack? "How do you keep at it even when you are not motivated?" may remind them why they keep at it to begin with. That gets closer to their purpose. Sound familiar? "You have not enough money. And how have you been managing to provide for your family as well as you have?" may invite them to take stock of what's working well despite the situation—to track their progress, see? By doing that, you remind them of the skills they already use to cope with undesired interactions and situations. Their competencies for creating small moments of success are accentuated. By the end of a brief encounter, people realize that they are much closer to what they want than they thought—a process called *resource activation* in communication research, or what I'd call *ordinary magic* in everyday life.

Reflection Guide

You may have heard of the term "ground zero." It can be defined as the center of intense change that reminds us of what happened, what used to be, and what could have been. Often it becomes the origin of our regrets and fears, even anger. But it doesn't end there. Ground zero also calls for us to remember, remind, and rebuild beyond what was lost into multiple possibilities.

- If you have had an experience of your life's ground zero, what was the greatest lesson you learned from going through it?

- What helped you through those moments of doubt, anger, and fear?

- If you might be going through it right now, what would you like this time to be remembered as after you are through it? What do you see this becoming?

Acknowledgments

PERHAPS IT BEGAN long before I was. Through my ancestors, my grandfathers that I've only met through layers of stories, my grandmothers who often told those stories. And perhaps it will continue long after I will be, becoming the beginning of another story or two for another generation or two. Stories become us as we make stories through us, and we become stories. In all our such connectedness, I acknowledge all who began, continued, and changed these stories as they found themselves in this tangible elaboration. I owe my soul-deep gratitude to all these relations:

Dad, you were alive when I started this. And as you ended your time here with hope, that was the last chapter I wrote. Thank you for leaving more than enough healing stories for my heart.

Mom, this book was already in the making when you taught me to write at four. You wrote in my journal every night of my childhood, and that love sustains me through the deepest and the darkest still.

Jamie and Calvin, my allies and confidants who keep me humble, mildly concerned, but mostly entertained. I love you—deal with it.

Bo Yon, my precious friend, you just know how to drive many winds out of my mind. My sounding board, guinea pig, and trusted advisor. The world would heal if everyone had a friend like you.

Peter De Jong, you opened my eyes and ears to how people make changes together in and through conversations. This book hopefully adds mouths to those eyes and ears so that the magic of Solution-Focused practice can be commonplace.

Peter Szabó, you ushered me into the world of facilitation. Your infectious joy of play inspired me to keep going and growing, discovering many stories shared in this book.

Ron, you introduced me to Solution-Focused counseling in that one summer course, and that changed my life. Thank you for that simple invitation to "go forth and make a difference."

Bailey, you carved out such needed time in my schedule to play, to rest, and to work. Without that intentional protection of my time, this book would have been just a mere dream still.

John, you refined not only my writing but also my identity as a writer. Your compliments were so genuine and sharp that my writer's soul was awakened.

Clients, from my early years till now, you've taught me how to coach. I'm still learning how to have better conversations with each of you each time.

Students, who've sat in my class trusting me with your time and experience, you've taught me how to teach. Your questions inspire me to aspire to be a better teacher. I remember those first few years of sitting in the parking lot beating myself up in total embarrassment, and you slowly taught me to get over myself.

And such an awesome team at Page Two who showed perpetual kindness, competence, and patience—Trena, Kendra, Jenny, Caela, Peter, Jennifer, Meghan, and many others who I'll continue to work with. Are you kidding? This book has your fingerprints all over it, including the potato guy that makes me smile every day.

It takes a village to write a book. It's my hope that this book will raise many more villages in your world in return. Thank you.

Resources

Video recordings

Better conversations: How to listen so that they will talk
[Video]. McMaster Alumni Talk. alumlc.org/mcmaster/6209

Creating meaning together: The power of dialogic intelligence
[Video]. CoachX lecture for the Institute of Coaching,
Affiliate of Harvard Medical School. vimeo.com/393719042

Powerful coaching [Video]. CoachX lecture for the Institute
of Coaching, Affiliate of Harvard Medical School.
instituteofcoaching.org/resources/coachx-haesun-moon-
powerful-coaching

Blogs

Coaching: Watching your language. Institute of Coaching
blog (2017, February 16). instituteofcoaching.org/blogs/
coaching-watching-your-language

Personal blog on Medium, medium.com/@haesun.moon

Books and articles

Coaching: Using ordinary words in extraordinary ways. In S. McNamee, M.M. Gergen, C. Camargo-Borges, and E.F. Rasera (Eds.), *The SAGE handbook of social constructionist practice* (pp. 246–257). SAGE Publications (2020).

Making progress visible for learners of solution-focused dialogue. *Solution Focused in Organisations*, 11(1), August 2019, 4. academia.edu/40084382/Making_Progress_Visible_for_Learners_of_Solution-Focused_Dialogue

The masterclass: A heutagogical approach to learning solution-focused conversation. *The InterAction collection of solution focus practice in organisations* 12 (2020). sfio.org/interaction/2020-1/a-heutagogical-approach-to-learning-sf-conversation

Thriving women, thriving world: An invitation to dialogue, healing, and inspired actions. Collaboration with Diana Whitney, Jessica Cocciolone, Caroline Adams Miller, et al. Taos Institute (2019). taosinstitute.net/product/thriving-women-thriving-world-an-invitation-to-dialogue-healing-and-inspired-actions

About the Author

HAESUN MOON, PhD, is a communication scientist, educator, and author of several collaborative books, including *Thriving Women, Thriving World*, and *Foundations of Brief Coaching*, a short handbook for professional coaches. Haesun received her PhD in Adult Education and Community Development from the University of Toronto. She cares about people experiencing better conversations at home and at work—and she does that by training, coaching, and consulting. She believes that conversations can change the world, and she defines this process as hosting dialogic conditions in which people participate to imagineer their own change. Her academic and professional research in coaching dialogues and pedagogy from the University of Toronto led to the development of a simple coaching model, the Dialogic Orientation Quadrant (DOQ). The DOQ has transformed the way people coach and learn coaching worldwide. Haesun teaches brief coaching at the University of Toronto, and she serves as executive director at the Canadian Centre for Brief Coaching and principal at the Human Learning Institute. When not writing, Haesun enjoys filmmaking, carpentry, and golf. A lover of early mornings, naps, good coffee, and fine pens with fine nibs, she currently resides in Toronto with her mother, her two nephews, and her exceptionally affectionate and independent dog, who failed her therapy dog program. You can visit her online at briefcoaching.ca and coachingatoz.com.

Share This Gift of Better Conversation

Good research tells good stories, and this book is full of them. As you read a story or two in the book, you probably remembered your own story or two. If you followed along slowly with the Reflection Guides, you may have had many stories merging and emerging. What if those stories are actually superpowers that you can use to restore, renew, or even reset your most important relationships?

A simple gift

This book was written with a specific intention to make that superpower accessible. Whether you wonder how to make conversations better at work or at home for yourself and others, this book is a simple gift to get started.

How you can share

Here are some ideas for how to best use this book:

- Buy a copy for someone who might appreciate it (or share yours!).

- Start or join a reading group with the Reading Guide available on coachingatoz.com.

- Write a review of the book on your favorite online book retailer's website or reading community.

- Share your emerging stories with me and with others.

- Host a learning event (webinar, virtual or in-person training, conference) for your team, organization, or community.

And there may be other ways that you are already sharing this gift with others. Thank you for doing that.

Stay connected

✉ learn@briefcoaching.ca
⊙ @CoachingAtoZ
⊕ coachingatoz.com